Understanding Shmittoh

Halochos of Shmittoh

FELDHEIM PUBLISHERS

Jerusalem | New York

Understanding Shmittoh

its sources and background

꩜꩜꩜꩜ & ꩜꩜꩜꩜꩜꩜꩜꩜꩜꩜꩜꩜꩜꩜꩜꩜

Halochos of Shmittoh

꩜꩜꩜꩜꩜꩜꩜꩜꩜꩜꩜꩜꩜꩜꩜꩜꩜꩜꩜꩜꩜꩜

by Rabbi Dovid Marchant

꩜꩜꩜꩜꩜꩜꩜꩜꩜꩜꩜꩜꩜꩜꩜꩜꩜꩜꩜꩜꩜

edited by Rabbi Noach Orlowek

꩜꩜꩜꩜꩜꩜꩜꩜꩜꩜꩜꩜꩜꩜꩜꩜꩜꩜꩜꩜꩜

Newly revised edition

꩜꩜꩜꩜꩜꩜꩜꩜꩜꩜꩜꩜꩜꩜꩜꩜꩜꩜꩜

ISBN 0-87306-425-9

Address:
12 Ezras Torah
Jerusalem
(02)- 383-243

FELDHEIM PUBLISHERS
POB 35002 / Jerusalem, Israel

200 Airport Executive Park
Spring Valley, NY 10977

Printed in Israel

...וְהָאֵר עֵינֵינוּ בְּתוֹרָתֶךָ וְדַבֵּק לִבֵּנוּ בְּמִצְוֹתֶיךָ, וְיַחֵד לְבָבֵנוּ לְאַהֲבָה וּלְיִרְאָה אֶת שְׁמֶךָ

מֶרְכַּז הַתּוֹרָה (ע)ש(הגר״ץ)
THE TORAH CENTRE

רב ונשיא
חכימה שטערנבוך שליט״א
על פי עיניים וזמנים (ע״ח) ועוד

לשמע ללמד וללמד
to hear, to learn, to teach . . . .

P.O. BOX 3131
JOHANNESBURG 2000
REP. OF SOUTH AFRICA.
TELEPHONE
(011) 648-5374

RAV & DIRECTOR
RABBI MOISHE STERNBUCH

[handwritten Hebrew text]

הן בא לפני אברך יקר ומופלג מאד בתו״י ומפואר לתהלה ה״ה הרב דוד
מרצ׳נט שליט״א, וסיפרו בידו לבאר היסודות דשמיטה לדוברי אנגלית, וכן
מעיקרי דיניה למעשה, ועיינתי מעט, וראיתי שדבריו נעימים, ויביאו ברכה
ותועלת מרובה למעיינים בו, ומצוה רבה קעביד להוציא מתחת ידו ספר
כמוהו. והנה סיבת גלותינו שזלזולו במצות שמיטה, וכל פעולה לעורר
הציבור בחשיבות המצוה מקרב גאולתינו, ומברך אני מאד המחבר המופלג
שליט״א שספרו יתפשש ויתבדר בארץ ובחו״ל, ורבים יהנו מאורו, ונותן
התורה הבורא ית״ש יצוה ברכתו שהגלית לשומרי שביעית, ובמהרה נלכה
לישועת ה׳ וגאולה שלימה.

ממני המצפה בכליון לישועת ה׳

משה שטרנבוך

Rabbi CHAIM P. SCHEINBERG

KIRYAT MATTERSDORF
PANIM MEIROT 2
JERUSALEM, ISRAEL

הרב חיים פנחס שיינברג
ראש ישיבת "תורה אור"
ומורה הוראה דקרית מטרסדורף
ירושלים טל.גו,ט,ט,ל

הנה בא לפני האברך היקר הרב דוד מרצ'נט שליט"א שאני
מכירו כבר מכמה שנים כירא שמים ובן תורה ובידו חיבור
מסודר על יסודות השמיטה בשפת האנגלית מיוסדים על
סוגיות הש"ס וביאורי הראשונים והאחרונים וניכר
עמלותו הכתבים. והנני רואה בזה תועלת לרבים, כיון
שבא לקרב עניני שמיטה לתודעת הצבור, ולא לפסוק הלכה
למעשה.

והריני לחזק בזה את ידיו ומברכו שיזכהו השי"ת לשבת
באהלה של תורה מתוך הרחבת הדעת להגדיל תורה
ולהאדירה.

נאום חיים פנחס שיינברג

TABLE OF CONTENTS

5. I am generally meticulous about separating Terumos and Ma'aseros from whatever I buy, even from a store with a hechsher for Terumos and Ma'aseros. Do I need to continue this during Shmittoh?

6. I am in a situation where I find that food prepared for me was cooked in pots which had previously been used for cooking forbidden vegetables. What am I to do?

7. May I buy flowers during Shmittoh?

8. What about tobacco in cigarettes?

9. How long after Shmittoh must I continue to be careful about what to buy?

1. How am I to treat leftovers of Shmittoh produce on my plate?

2. May I wash off plates and clean out pots which have scrapings of Shmittoh produce sticking to them?

3. Is it preferable to cook and serve an amount of Shmittoh produce that I think will not be leftover?

4. What course of action must be taken when giving young infants Shmittoh produce, such as bananas, which they usually make a mess of?

5. I have used Shmittoh produce merely as flavouring for soup, meat, or fish. How am I to treat this food?

6. When peeling Shmittoh apples and the like, do I have to be careful to minimize the thickness of the peel?

7. What does one do with the pips from Shmittoh produce?

8. May I puree or extract the juice from Shmittoh produce?

9. Wine and grape juice evaporate when they are boiled. Is it forbidden to use wine or grape juice which have kedushas shviyis, in cooking?

7. I have pickled (or cooked) various Shmittoh produce together so that they all have the taste of each other in them. When the time for biyur arrives for one of them, do I have to remove all of them, since the taste of it is in them?

8. I sold a friend of mine a couple of apples (selling Shmittoh produce on such a small scale is permitted) which have kedushas shviyis. The coins given to me have the kedushas shviyis of the apples in them. When the date of biyur for apples comes, is it necessary for me to do biyur on these coins?

9. I keep the custom to consider Shmittoh produce grown in a non-Jewish domain in Eretz Yisroel as having kedushas shviyis. Do I have to remove them just like produce grown in a Jewish domain?

Chapter five: COMMERCIAL DEALINGS   193

1. My only opportunity at the moment is to buy my fruit from a store where they do not observe hilchos Shmittoh. Is there anyway I can deal with this situation?

2. Is it permitted to sell Shmittoh produce by weight (so much for a kilogram) volume or number (so many for the shekel)? Would such a procedure turn it into a business transaction?

3. If I am selling Shmittoh produce in the permitted manner, the money I receive has kedushas shviyis. When I buy food with it, may I buy it from an Am Ha'oretz?

4. If money only loses kedushas shviyis if exchanged for food and drink then it means that those who do not adhere to this halocha, and use the money for other purposes, cause markets and banks etc to be flooded with money having kedushas shviyis. Does this mean that when I take out money from the bank or receive change from commodity shops I can only spend it on food and drink?

PREFACE

״רבות מחשבות בלב איש ועצת ה׳ היא תקום״
(משלי יט:כא)

"Many thoughts are in man's heart, but the counsel of Hashem—only it will prevail."

People make all sorts of plans; people plan all sorts of good and righteous undertakings. As much as it is Hashem's will that we make these plans and try to see them through to fruition, not even the slightest or simplest project can have any success at all unless Hashem wills it so.

Countless times it was clear that without the *siyate dishmayoh,* the best laid plans for writing and publishing this sefer would have come to naught.

I wish to use this privilege to praise Hashem for having given me the privilege to praise Him in public. ״הודו לה׳ כי טוב כי לעולם חסדו״

"Understanding Shmittoh" consists of two parts. One part, "Shmittoh in General", is intended to give a brief and basic understanding of Shmittoh. The second part, "Shmittoh in Depth", provides a detailed analysis of Shmittoh in a step by step fashion. First by giving the sources as found in the Chumash, Mishnayos, Toras Kohanim, and Gemoros, then by an analysis of the logic behind the sources. Finally, the opinions of the Rishonim are offered. Several Achronim, notably the Chazon Ish, also provide important information.

It is therefore hoped that those who themselves may not be able to make an in-depth study of these sources will be able to obtain a deeper understanding of Shmittoh in a shorter amount of time.

The Hebrew sources which have been quoted here are of benefit to anyone wishing to make his own research of the subject, and thus this sefer may be used as a stepping stone for further study.

Although the idea has been to present more detailed information on the Shmittoh year than has been found so far available to the English speaking public, nevertheless it must be understood that it is beyond the scope of such a work to bring every opinion and to answer all apparent contradictions which may be found in the commentaries.

Care was taken not to mention any extraneous sources. Many ideas, however, were introduced in order to aid the person who is involved in a particular sugya (topic) and will assist him in understanding some particularly complex point. In addition, due to the connection of some parts of the subject, notably the melochos, to Hilchos Shabbos, information was added to assist those making a study of the melochos of Shabbos.

The two parts, "Shmittoh in General" and "Shmittoh in Depth" are connected. "Shmittoh in General" contains brackets containing a number with an asterisk next to it. This number refers to a more detailed analysis of the subject, appearing in "Shmittoh in Depth", in the corresponding chapter.

Several topics, notably doing business with Shmittoh produce, household treatment and *biyur* of Shmittoh produce were discussed mainly in the sefer dealing with practical halocho due to their pertinence to day-to-day halocha.

The halocha section is according to the p'sakim of Hagaon Harav Moishe Sternbuch Shlita references are made to his sefer שמיטה כהלכתה I felt that a question and answer format would more effectively convey the halocha to the reader, to which Harav Sternbuch also gave his approval. Intended here as a separate sefer, apart from "Understanding Shmittoh", it gives much practical insight into the day-to-day application of the laws of Shmittoh.

I wish to take this opportunity to thank the following persons, who gave unstintingly to this sefer, with time and encouragement.

First and foremost my wife Chana מנב״ח, a true Aishes Chayil whose devotion and self sacrifice enables me to devote myself to a full time learning schedule. It can· truly be said "שלי ושלכם שלה הוא"

Special gratitude is owed to the Rabbeim in the various yeshivos which I have attended throughout the years. In particular the late Mirrer Rosh Yeshiva, Moreinu Ve'Rabbeinu HaRav Chaim Shmuelevitz זצללה״ה who was a paragon in word and deed of assiduos Torah learning. HaGaon HaRav Binyomin Beinush Finkel זצללה״ה the late Mirrer Rosh Yeshiva, who with self sacrifice was a sheliach of Hashem in providing as much parnosah as possible for hundreds of our Yeshivaleit שתחי׳ is deserving of my special thanks. Deepest thanks goes to HaGaon Harav Chaim Dov Altusky Shlita for his time in looking through the original manuscript of "Understanding Shmittoh".

A special thanks to HaGaon HaRav Moishe Sternbuch Shlita for his great interest and encouragement, also for giving me his permission to base the section "Halochos of Shmittoh" on his sefer שמיטה כהלכתה. My gratitude also goes to HaRav Yissochor Shreiber Shlita who gave me valuable advice.

I deeply appreciate the hard and enthusiastic work which Mrs. Nechama Berg and Miss Bina Emanuel put into typing and making this sefer ready·for print.

Short words can barely express my gratitude to my friend HaRav Noach Orlowek Shlita not only editor of this sefer but with complete self sacrifice criticized and with deep insight arranged the contents, making it readable to the public.

SHMITTOH

IN

GENERAL

All square brackets with an asterisk indicate to make reference to the same chapter found in ''Shmittoh in Depth'', (the latter part of this sefer) the number inside the brackets corresponds to the number in that chapter under which the subject matter is to be found.

CHAPTER ONE

SHMITTOH AND YOVEL

1. Defining "Shviyis" and "Shmittoh"

The word "Shviyis" literally means "seventh" and the Torah uses this term in commanding us that every seventh year we are to cease doing various forms of agricultural work in Eretz Yisroel, as it says,[1] "ובשנה השביעית שבת שבתון יהיה לארץ" "but in the seventh year there shall be a rest to the land".[יא] The word "Shmittoh" is used by the Torah to describe this cessation of work during the seventh year as it says[2] "והשביעית תשמטנה", "but the seventh year you shall let it rest". It is also used by the Torah to express that there must be at some stage during the Shmittoh year a cancelling of having to repay money borrowed, as it says[3] "מקץ שבע שנים תעשה שמיטה" "at the end of seven years you shall make a cancellation".

We therefore find that the Tannoim spoke of the seventh year as the Shmittoh year.[4] Thus the seventh year is popularly referred to as Shmittoh.

2. The First Shmittoh Year

When did the Am Yisroel first become obligated to observe the Shmittoh year?

HaShem told Moshe Rabbeinu on Har Sinai to instruct the Am Yisroel as follows[5] "כי תבואו אל הארץ אשר אני נותן לכם ושבתה הארץ שבת לד'...ובשנה השביעית שבת שבתון יהיה לארץ..." "when you come into the land which I give you, then the land shall rest in honour of HaShem...but in the seventh year there shall be a rest to the land...[5a]"

Thus, the Am Yisroel were commanded that when they will come

---

1. ויקרא כה: ד 2. שמות כג: יא 3. דברים טו: א 4. ראש השנה פ״א מ״א ״באחד בתשרי ראש השנה לשנים ולשמיטין״ 5. ויקרא כה: ב וד 5a. לפי פירש״י

into the Land promised to them by HaShem[6] they are to observe the Shmittoh year,[2*] which means that they were to begin counting a seven year cycle, the "Shmittoh Cycle", the seventh year being the Shmittoh year.

The area of land which was promised is referred to as Eretz Yisroel. Am Yisroel, led by Yehoshua, crossed over the Jordan river into this land on the 10th of Nisson 2488.[7] However, the obligation of counting the Shmittoh Cycle could not commence until fourteen years later, for the following reason:

3. Kedushas haOretz—The Sanctity of The Land

There is a rule concerning those agricultural mitzvos which apply specifically to Eretz Yisroel, *(Mitzvos Hateluyos B'oretz)* such as the mitzvoh of Shmittoh, that they are only obligatory during a time when there is what is referred to as *Kedushas haOretz.*[8] That is, although Eretz Yisroel was imbued with an intrinsic kedusha[9] (sanctity) from the time of Creation, nevertheless an additional level of kedusha was needed before the obligation to keep these agricultural mitzvos could begin. When the Am Yisroel entered the Land they took seven years to conquer it and become the ruling power.[10] This is referred to as *Kivush* (conquest), and it was this conquest which imbued the Land with a higher level of kedusha,[(1)] and caused the obligation to observe the mitzvoh of the Shmittoh

---

(1)It is explained[10a] that when the Torah elsewhere[10b] says ״כל המקום אשר תדרך כף רגלכם״ "every place where the sole of your feet will tread" this tells us that the conquest by the Am Yisroel of any land outside of Eretz Yisroel gives the land this special kedusha. (See Rambam תרומות פ״א for details) It is therefore possible to conclude (as the Rambam does[10c]) that the conquest of Eretz Yisroel certainly gives it this kedusha.

---

6. בראשית יב: ז 7. יהושע ד: יט 8. מתוך דברי הרמב״ם בית הבחירה פ״ו הל׳ ט״ז 9. עי׳ רמב״ם שם פ״ז ריש הל׳ י״ב 10. יהושע יד: ז׳־י׳ ועי׳ ערכין יג. 10a. תוס׳ גיטין ח. ד״ה ״כיבוש״ 10b. דברים יא: כד 10c. בית הבחירה פ״ו הל׳ ט״ז ותרומות פ״א הל׳ ה׳.

year and all the other various agricultural mitzvos.[11] However, on account of another condition which was lacking at that time, they were not yet obligated in this mitzvoh even though the Land had the required kedusha.[12] What was this condition?

4. Chalukas haOretz—Division of The Land

The Torah[13] speaks of "שדך" "your field(you shall not sow)" and "כרמך" "your vineyard (you shall not prune)". In order for the Am Yisroel to finally become obligated to observe the mitzvoh of the Shmittoh year, Eretz Yisroel had to be recognized as being owned by the individual Jew so that one could say to him "this is *your* field", "this is *your* vineyard".[14] It took seven years after the conquest to divide the land between the twelve tribes and their individual families,[15] each person being then able to recognize which area of land personally belonged to him and thereby be referred to as "*your* field", "*your* vineyard".

After this initial fourteen year period (termed *Sheva Shekovshu Ve'sheva Shechilku),* ending the 10th of Nisson 2502, the Am Yisroel could begin counting the Shmittoh Cycle. Since the cycle can only begin from Rosh Hashona,[16] the count began from the first of Tishrei of the following year, 2503.[17(2)] The very first Shmittoh year therefore began on the first of Tishrei 2509.[(3)]

5. Yovel

The Torah[18] commands us to count seven years (one Shmittoh

(2) The Rambam[17a] explains that the year 2503 dates from the beginning of the *second* year after the creation of Adom haRishon, therefore being year 2504 from the day of his actual creation (Rosh Hashona). The Shmittoh year being the year 2510 from his creation (ibid). Both Rambam and Toras Kohanim[17b] state that this first Shmittoh year was the twenty-first year from the entry of Am Yisroel into the land (2488). This is therefore considering the Shmittoh as having been year 2509, Nisson of this year completing the twenty-one years.

(3) See footnote (2).

11. רמב״ם בית הבחירה שם וע״ע תרומות שם 12. משמעות דברי תורת כהנים ריש פרשת בהר ורמב״ם תרומות שם ובית הבחירה שם 13. ויקרא כה: ג־ד 14. על פי תורת כהנים שם 15. ערכין יג. 16. לפי משמעות מפירש״י ערכין יג. סוף ד״ה ״וכתיב ושיציא ביתא״. וכן כתב הרמב״ם שמיטה ויובל פ״י הל׳ ד׳ 17. רמב״ם שם הל׳ ב׳ 17a. שם 17b. שם 18. ויקרא כה: ח

Cycle) seven times i.e. forty-nine years, the forty ninth year being a Shmittoh year.

The fiftieth year commences what is termed as the Yovel. The Torah gave the name "Yovel" to the fiftieth year so that it would have a special name of its own, thus being distinguished from all the other years.[19] It was given the name "Yovel" because[20] this is the name for the ram's horn[21] which is to be sounded on Yom Kippur of the Yovel year[22] to announce the return of fields to their original owners and the freeing of slaves.[23] In addition, the Yovel year is to be like the Shmittoh year, in that the land must rest from having work done to it.[24] Therefore, being that the Yovel year follows a Shmittoh year, this means that there would be a cessation of work on the land for two consecutive years—the forty-ninth year (Shmittoh) and the fiftieth year (Yovel).[25][3*]

6. Conditions for the observance of Yovel

There are two conditions required to cause an obligation to observe the Yovel year:[4*]

(A) All of the Am Yisroel, or according to some opinions,[4*]a *representation* of each of the tribes, must be living in Eretz Yisroel.

(B) The Land must be inhabited in the manner designated at the time of the division of the Land (see above, no. 4) that is, each tribe inhabiting their own area of land and not that they are living in a mixed fashion, such as the tribe of Binyomin inhabiting the area assigned to the tribe of Yehudah, or visa versa.

The first of Tishrei 2552 marked the beginning of the first Yovel year, forty-nine years having elapsed from the first of Tishrei 2503 when the Shmittoh Cycles first began to be counted.[4]

(4) The Toras Kohanim (ibid) and Rambam (ibid) explain that in Nisson of this year sixty-four years had passed since the entry into Eretz Yisroel.

CHAPTER TWO

SHMITTOH THROUGH THE AGES

1. The Exile of The Ten Tribes

During the reign of Sancheriv King of Ashur, the last of the ten tribes were exiled, in the year 3205.[1] This process had begun nine years earlier with the tribes Reuven, Gad, and half of Menashe who were living in Ever Hayarden.[2(1)] Only the tribes of Yehudah and Binyomin remained living in Eretz Yisroel. No longer did all of the Am Yisroel live in Eretz Yisroel and Ever Hayarden, and therefore there was no longer an obligation to observe the Yovel year (see Chapter One no. 6). Due to the fact that there is a dispute amongst the Tannoim as to whether or not the obligation to observe the Shmittoh year is dependent on there being an obligation to observe the Yovel year, (Chapter One[5*]), it is therefore questionable if the tribes of Yehudah and Binyomin, who remained living in Eretz Yisroel, observed the Shmittoh year midorysa (as a Torah obligation) or miderabbonon (as a Rabbinical obligation).

In the year 3303, ninety-eight years after the ten tribes had been exiled, the prophet Yirmiyohu brought to Eretz Yisroel persons from each of the exiled tribes.[3] From then, until the destruction of the First Bais haMikdosh, the laws applying to the Yovel year were observed, since now there were in Eretz Yisroel at least a representative of each tribe.[2]

---

(1) For details of Ever Hayarden see "Shmittoh in Depth" Chapter One footnote (1).
(2) Whether they observed it midorysa or miderabbonon is a dispute amongst the Rishonim (see "Shmittoh in Depth" Chapter One footnote (8).

1. רש"י מלכים ב, יז: א 2. רש"י שם ועוד בגיטין מז: ד"ה "המוכר שדהו לפירות" ועי' ערכין לב:
3. רש"י ירמיה ג: יב

2. Kedushas haOretz and Kedushas Yerushalayim VehaBayis—The Sanctification of The Land and the Sanctification of Yerushalayim and the Bais haMikdosh.

The kedusha which Yehoshua established by way of conquest (see Chapter One no. 3) is referred to as the *Kedusha Rishona* (first kedusha). Later, another special kedusha was established in the area of the Bais haMikdosh and Yerushalayim by Dovid haMelech and his son Shlomo haMelech,[4] and it is also referred to as being a *Kedusha Rishona*. This kedusha, however, had nothing to do with creating the obligation of Shmittoh[5] which had been in effect due to the kedusha established in the time of Yehoshua.

Thus there was a *Kedusha Rishona* established in the whole area of Eretz Yisroel for the obligation of Shmittoh which is referred to as *Kedushas haOretz* and another *Kedusha Rishona* was established in the area of Yerushalayim and the Bais haMikdosh which is referred to as *Kedushas Yerushalayim VehaBayis*.

3. Kedusha Rishona Kidsha L'Sheita or Kidsha L'Sheita Vel'osid L'vo

In the Gemora[6] the question is posed as to whether the *Kedusha Rishona* was of a permanent nature or would only last as long as the Am Yisroel maintained their sovereignty over Eretz Yisroel.[1*] It is a dispute amongst the Tannoim[7] which way to decide this question[1*] and this is similarly disputed amongst the Geonim and the Rishonim.[8][2*]

The destruction of the First Bais haMikdosh took place on the 9th

4. עי׳ רש״י שבועות טז. ד״ה ״רב הונא וכו׳״ 5. מתוך דברי הרמב״ם בית הבחירה פ״ו הל׳ ט״ז 6. שבועות טז. חולין ז. ועוד מקומות 7. ערכין לב: 8. עי׳ רמב״ם שם ושמיטה ויובל פ״י הל׳ ה׳ ותוס׳ יבמות פב: ד״ה ״ירושה״

of Av in the year 3338.[9] Consequently the Am Yisroel lost their sovereignty in Eretz Yisroel and were exiled to Bovel (Babylonia) by Nevuchadnetzar. According to the opinion that the *Kedushas haOretz* only existed as long as the Am Yisroel retained their sovereignty over Eretz Yisroel, then it was this exile which caused the nullification of this kedusha since the sovereignty no longer remained.[10] Therefore there was no longer any obligation either midorysa or miderabbonon to observe the Shmittoh year.[3*] The *Kedusha Rishona* of Yerushalayim and the Bais haMikdosh did not become nullified.[11][4*]

4. Kedusha Shniya—The Second Sanctification

According to the opinion that the *Kedushas haOretz* was only temporarily established and became nullified after the destruction of the First Bais haMikdosh [1,2*] then it means that when the Am Yisroel returned to Eretz Yisroel there was an establishment of another kedusha to the land, termed *Kedusha Shniya*. After seventy years[12] of having laid in ruins the rebuilding of the Second Bais haMikdosh commenced. This construction[3] took place in the second year of the reign of Daryovesh, in the year 3408.[13] It was completed four years later,[14] in the year 3412. A year later, in 3413, Ezra haSofer came from Bovel to Yerushalayim[15] and by the time of his arrival it was already the month of Av 3414, six years having elapsed since the beginning of the reconstruction.[4] He established a kedusha which re-established the obligation to observe the Shmittoh year.

This *Kedusha Shniya* was established by way of *Chazoka,* [16] meaning that the Am Yisroel imbued the land with this kedusha by

---

(3) Which resumed once again after having been previously halted.[12a]

(4) This is according to Rashi.[15a] The Rambam[15b] however appears to dispute this in stating that Ezra came up from Bovel in the seventh year after the reconstruction.[15c]

9. מלכים ב, כה: ח 10. רמב״ם תרומות פ״א הל׳ ה׳ ובבית הבחירה פ״ו הל׳ ט״ו 11. רמב״ם בית הבחירה שם 12. דניאל ט׳: ב 12a. עי׳ עזרא ד 13. עזרא ד: כד 14. עזרא ו: טו ועי׳ פירש״י 15. עזרא ז: ז ועי׳ פירש״י 15a. רש״י ערכין יג. ד״ה ״וכתיב שיציא ביתא״ 15b. רמב״ם שמיטה ויובל פ״י הל׳ ג׳ 15c. וכן כתב רדב״ז שם 16. רמב״ם בית הבחירה פ״ו סוף הל׳ ט״ז

virtue of their living there. They did not become the ruling power and therefore this *Kedusha Shniya* existed without conquest.

According to the Rambam[17] this *Kedusha Shniya* of the land was established to last forever, even should there come a time when the Am Yisroel would no longer be living on the land [5] *(Kedusha Shniya Kidsha L'Sheita and Kidsha L'osid L'vo).*

Although there was now the existence of this *Kedusha Shniya,* they did not begin to count the Shmittoh Cycle until the first of Tishrei 3415,[18] which marked the beginning of the seventh year from the commencement of the reconstruction of the Second Bais haMikdosh.[6] Therefore, after the elapse of six years (beginning the thirteenth year from the commencement of the construction of the Second Bais haMikdosh) there was a Shmittoh year.[19][5*]

5. Period of The Second Bais haMikdosh

When Ezra haSofer returned from the exile in Bovel he brought back with him descendants of those representatives of each tribe who were originally brought back by Yirmiyohu (see above, no. 1) and were re-exiled to Bovel, therefore once again there were present those conditions necessary to renew the obligation to observe both the Shmittoh and Yovel years [6*] (see Chapter One no. 6). Whether these obligations were midorysa or miderabbonon is a subject of dispute.[7*]

(5) The question is asked by the Kesef Mishna[17a]—how could this *Kedusha Shniya* which came by way of *Chazoka* without conquest have more of a lasting effect than the *Kedusha Rishona* which came by way of Chazoka *with* conquest? The Kesef Mishna remains with this question.

(6) The Rambam[18a] appears to agree on this point by stating that they counted from the beginning of the seventh year after the reconstruction. The Radvaz however appears to understand that the Rambam here means to say that they began to count from the following year(3416). This, however, would contradict the next statement of the Rambam that the Shmittoh year was the *thirteenth* year from the reconstruction.

17. תרומות פ״א הל׳ ה׳ 17a. כסף משנה בית הבחירה פ״ו הל׳ ט״ז 18. רש״י ערכין יג. ד״ה וכתיב ושיציא ביתא 18a. רמב״ם שמיטה ויובל פ״י הל׳ ג׳ 19. עי׳ רמב״ם שם

6. The Destruction of The Second Bais haMikdosh

After having stood for a period of four hundred and twenty years,[20] the Second Bais haMikdosh was destroyed on the ninth of Av 3828. Two months after this, the first of Tishrei 3829, was Motzoai Shmittoh.[21(7)]

As already mentioned, according to the view of the Rambam that the *Kedusha Shniya* of the land was established to exist forever, this means that even after the destruction of the Second Bais haMikdosh until today there is an obligation to observe the Shmittoh year. This is also the opinion of the Bais Yosef.[22] However it is questionable as to whether we are observing its laws as an obligation midorysa or miderabbonon (this being dependant on the individual views of Rebbi and the Rabbonon, Chapter One [5*]).

The Chazon Ish [23] writes that concerning the Shmittoh year nowadays, it can be relied upon that it is an obligation miderabbonon since this is the opinion of the Rambam,[24] being that he paskens like Rebbi.

Also, being that according to the Rambam and the Geonim[2*] the *Kedusha Rishona* of Kedushas Yerushalayim and the Bais haMikdosh never became nullified, therefore it is forbidden for us today to enter the area of the Bais haMikdosh since we are ritually

---

(7) Beginning with the seventh year after the commencement of the building of the Second Bais haMikdosh, they began the count of the Shmittoh Cycle.[21a] Therefore in subtracting those first 6 years from 420 years we come to the figure 414 years of counting Shmittoh and Yovel. According to the Rabbonon who do not count the Yovel year as part of the following Shmittoh Cycle,[3*] then it means that this 414 years is divided by 50, this brings us to a total of 8 Yovel years with a remainder of 14 years, thus this 14th year in which the destruction occurred was a Shmittoh year, and the very next year being the beginning of the 15th year of the Yovel Cycle[21b] was Motzoai Shmittoh.

---

unclean and any intentional transgression of this prohibition carries with it the punishment of *Misoh Bidey Shomayim.* [25(8)]

7. The Calculation Today

The Rambam[26] in accordance with the Geonim writes that from the time of the destruction of the Second Bais haMikdosh the count of the Shmittoh Cycle has been made by counting seven yearly periods one after the other without the inclusion of the count of Yovel years. The first year of this manner of counting was from the beginning of the year following the destruction of the Second Bais haMikdosh[(9)] the lst of Tishrei 3829. Therefore the 1st of Tishrei 5754 completes 1925 years from the 1st of Tishrei 3829. The year 5754 is therefore the 275th Shmittoh year following the destruction of the Second Bais haMikdosh.

(8) A premature death.[25a] Even though Shmittoh is miderabbonon nevertheless this is only on account of the lack of conditions necessary for the obligation of Yovel (see Chapter One no.6), something which does not affect the strength of the prohibition in the area of the Mikdosh which therefore carries with it such severe punishment.
(9) As mentioned above, this was Motzoai Shmittoh which was the beginning of a new seven year Shmittoh Cycle.

25. עי' רמב"ם ביאת המקדש פ"ג הל' י"ב וי"ג 25a. עי' ירושלמי ביכורים פ"ב ובבלי מועד קטן כח.
26. שמיטה ויובל פ"י הל' ו'

CHAPTER THREE

THE MELOCHOS

1. Defining "Melocha"

As mentioned in Chapter One (no. 1), various forms of agricultural work are prohibited in Eretz Yisroel during the Shmittoh year. These forms of work are called *melochos.*

The term "melocha" is found in the Torah with regard to Shabbos "מלאכה כל" [1] "ויום השביעי שבת...לא תעשה כל מלאכה" "and the seventh day is Shabbos....You shall not do any work (melocha)". The Mishna [2] teaches that there are thirty-nine principal melochos which the Torah here is forbidding us to do on Shabbos. The Gemora [3] derives these melochos from the various types of work which were required for the construction of the Mishkon. The Torah [4] purposely mentioned the observance of Shabbos in juxtaposition to the construction of the Mishkon in order to tell us that these are the melochos which the Torah forbids on Shabbos.

The Torah here has thereby clearly defined for us that what is meant by "you shall not do any *work*" is that "work" is not defined by the degree of physical exertion but in its similarity to those activities needed in constructing the Mishkon.

2. Av Melocha and Toldah

There are two terms which Chazal use in connection with the melochos of both Shabbos and Shmittoh. These are "Av Melocha" (lit: father, or primary melocha) and "Toldah" (lit: offspring or derivative of a primary melocha.[5])[(1)][(1*)]

(1) The idea behind a primary melocha determines what melochos are the derivatives.

1. שמות כ: י, דברים ה: יד 2. שבת פ״ז מ״ב 3. שבת מט: לפי פירש״י ד״ה ״כנגד עבודות המשכן״
4. שמות לה: ב, תעיין רש״י ביצה יג: ד״ה ״אלא מאי אית לך למימר״ 5. עיין רש״י שבת ע: ד״ה ״מהנה לרבות תולדות״

3. The Melochos of Shmittoh

Unlike Shabbos, the Torah concerning Shmittoh does not forbid melochos in a general way such as "לא תעשה מלאכה" ''you shall not do work''. It rather specifies the forbidden melochos—"שדך לא [6]תזרע וכרמך לא תזמר, את ספיח קצירך לא תקצור ואת ענבי...לא תבצור" ''your field you shall not sow and your vineyard you shall not prune. The S'fiach(2) you shall not reap (detaching produce from its source of growth[7]), the grapes...you shall not pick''. Thus the Torah lists four types of melochos which are forbidden during the Shmittoh year:-

1) zore'a—sowing seeds in soil
2) zomer—pruning
3) kotzer—reaping grains and legumes[8]
4) botzer—picking grapes[9]

Generally the Torah expresses ideas and laws which are meant as a prototype, the posuk stating a principle from which similar ideas are derived.[1*] This would normally mean that these four forms of work are merely prototypes from which derivative forms of work (Toldos) will be determined. In Hilchos Shabbos, these Toldos carry with them the same midorysa prohibition as the work specified in the posuk, while with regard to Shmittoh, this is not necessarily so, there being concerning this a debate amongst the Amoroim. [2*]

The Rambam[10] concludes that the Torah gives a positive commandment to refrain from all agricultural melochos—"ושבתה [11]הארץ שבת לד'" ''and the land shall rest in honour of Hashem'' and "בחריש ובקציר תשבות" [12]''from involvement in ploughing and reaping you shall rest''. With regard to a negative commandment, the Rambam[13] decides according to the opinion of Rabbi Yochonon, [2*] that only the four melochos—zore'a, zomer, kotzer and botzer are

(2) See Chapter Six.

6. ויקרא כה: ד־ה עם פירש״י 7. שבת קז: 8. רמב״ם שבת פ״ז הל׳ ד׳ 9. רמב״ם שם 10. שמיטה ויובל פ״א הל׳ א׳ 11. ויקרא כה: ב 12. שמות לד: כא 13. שם הל׳ ב וג׳

prohibited *midorysa*. There is, however a prohibition *miderabbonon* on all other agricultural *melochos* and the Rabbonon themselves have instituted the penalty of *malkus* (lashes dealt out by the Bais Din) for anyone transgressing these *melochos* during the Shmittoh year.

4. Melocha Indoors

Although the four *melochos* specifically referred to in the *posuk* are *melochos* usually done outdoors, in a field or vineyard, nevertheless under certain circumstances *melocha* during Shmittoh could also be prohibited indoors.[3*] The earthen floor of a home or plants grown in flowerpots can sometimes be included in the Torah's prohibition of *melocha* during Shmittoh.[3,4*]

5. Shmittoh Melochos Performed Unintentionally (דבר שאינו מתכוין)

In areas of Torah such as in Hilchos Shmittoh we pasken like Rabbi Shimon that prohibitions done unintentionally(דבר שאינו מתכוין) are not considered a violation, only intention (דבר המתכוין) for the act is a Torah violation.[5*]

6. Shmittoh Melochos concerning Meleches Machsheves

In discussing the construction of the Mishkon the Torah[14] mentions the term *Meleches Machsheves* [5*] (purposeful *melocha*). On account of this, Rabbi Yehudah understands that in order to be forbidden *midorysa* as a *melocha* on Shabbos the action must be done with *machshova* (intention).[15(3)] Shmittoh *melocha*, however, has no such condition.[16] Due to this difference between Shabbos

---

(3) According to Rabbi Shimon *Meleches Machsheves* in Hilchos Shabbos creates a requirement of מלאכה שצריכה לגופה (see no. (7), as far as דבר המתכוין is concerned then even without *Meleches Machsheves* he understands (as in other areas of Torah) that *melocha* done unintentionally is not a violation.

and Shmittoh some Rishonim[17] suggest that there is a resulting leniency in Hilchos Shmittoh.

For example,[18] if one cuts branches from a tree intending to use the wood and he cuts them in a fashion that does not enhance tree growth (i.e. it is not a melocha of zomer), nevertheless if this was done on Shabbos it would be the melocha of kotzer (detaching a product from its source of growth[19]), because although his action here is not kotzer (since he is merely chopping wood which is not the *product* of a fruit tree) nevertheless *Meleches Machsheves* tells us that awareness, consciousness, of doing the melocha (*machshova*) plays a role in making it into a melocha (i.e. that action alone is not enough but requires awareness, that it not be done unwittingly.) Therefore being that he had the intention here to use the wood, this *machshova* has helped to categorize the wood as a form of *produce* of the tree and thus considered as having done the melocha of kotzer. However if this is done during Shmittoh where there is no involvement of *Meleches Machsheves*, so that being considered melocha is *not* dependent on *machshova* one has, but merely on the *action* he does, then his *machshova* here to use the wood does not help to make it into the melocha of kotzer, (being that the wood, without introducing his *machshova*, is not normally considered *produce* of the tree and hence cannot be kotzer) rather he is considered as merely chopping wood which is not a melocha. Therefore even though he does this action with intention it is permitted even according to Rabbi Shimon.[4]

7. **Shmittoh Melochos concerning** מלאכה שצריכה לגופה [5*]

Rabbi Shimon is of the opinion that even without *Meleches Machsheves* one must have intention for an act in order for it to be a

---

(4) See "Halachos of Shmittoh" Chapter One no. 13.

17. עייו תוס׳ סנהדרין כו. ד״ה ״לעקל״ לפי פירוש המהרש״א 18. תוס׳ שם 19. שבת קז:

Torah violation. *Meleches Machsheves* in his opinion, however, comes to tell us that for an act on Shabbos to be considered a Torah violation it must be done for the same purpose for which it was needed in the Mishkon, termed מלאכה שצריכה לגופה.[5*] The melochos of Shmittoh are neither involved with *Meleches Machsheves* nor with the Mishkon. Therefore, Rabbi Shimon agrees (unlike in Hilchos Shabbos) that the definition of melocha is only *action,* the fact that one is not intent on the purpose of the action (i.e. it is a מלאכה שאינו צריכה לגופה) is of no consequence. Thus a situation is possible where one does a melocha which although done on Shabbos it is not considered a violation, nevertheless if done during Shmittoh it is a violation.

For example,[20] if one picks thorns from his field and by doing this he definitely (פסיק רישא)[5*] improves the ground, (the purpose, the צריכה לגופה, of the melocha of ploughing in the Mishkon) then even though he did not intend to plough (he wanted the thorns for some use), nevertheless since it is a פסיק רישא then it is considered as having been intended (דבר המתכוין). However if he has done this in another person's field then it is a case of where he has no personal benefit, לא ניחה ליה,[5*] and therefore it is not evident that he has intended to do the melocha for the purpose of having an improved soil. Therefore concerning Hilchos Shabbos it is a מלאכה שאינה צריכה לגופה and has not been considered a Torah violation. However concerning Hilchos Shmittoh where being צריכה לגופה is not a factor[5] then as long as his action is considered intentional (because of פסיק רישא) then it is forbidden.

---

(5) Tosfos[20a] mentions *Meleches Machsheves* as the missing factor to make it מלאכה שצריכה לגופה, even though the mere lack of Mishkon is enough to say there is no involvement of מלאכה שצריכה לגופה in Hilchos Shmittoh? Either this is a different בעל תוס׳ (from Tosfos in שבת צד. ד״ה ״רבי״) who understands that מלאכה שצריכה לגופה only involves *Meleches Machsheves* and not Mishkon (like רש״י שבת צג:) or תוס׳ here is לאו דוקא.

20. עיין תוס׳ גיטין מד: ד״ה ״שנתקוצה״ 20a. מועד קטן ג. ד״ה ״נטיבה.״

A common application of this (albeit in a derabbonon context[6]) is where one washes his hands over plants or grass. This will definitely cause growth (פסיק רישא) and therefore this act of watering plants is considered intentional (דבר המתכוין), and even though he does not care (לא ניחה ליה) about having the plants it is still forbidden.[21] [6a]

8. When melocha is permitted during Shmittoh

The Gemora[22] tells us that in the Rabbonon having forbidden all other melochos concerning trees they only did so if the melocha is being done for "אברויי אילנא". That is, where the melocha causes the tree to become stronger and healthier (בריא) and improves it.[23] Where the melocha is being done for "אוקמי אילנא" i.e. it prevents the tree from deterioration or loss,[24] and thereby helps it to remain the way it is (מוקם) but does not *improve* the tree,[25] then it is permitted (providing that the אוקמי אילנא will not lead to אברויי אילנא, in which case it is forbidden).[26] There is a great discussion amongst the Achronim as to exactly when אוקמי אילנא is permitted. A shai'las chochom (specific question posed to a Halachic authority) must be asked with regard to the accepted halocha.

9. More about Kotzer

The prohibition to reap or pick is in some instances[7] not entirely prohibited, but what the Torah means to forbid is only reaping or

(6) Watering plants is a Toldah of zore'a (sowing: see "Shmittoh in Depth" chart of agricultural melochos)—such a Toldah during Shmittoh as far as a negative commandment is concerned is miderabbonon.[2*]

(6a) The Chazon Ish[21a] however brings a proof from the Yerushalmi disputing the view of Tosfos that there is no din of *Meleches Machsheves* concerning Hilchos Shmittoh, and therefore is of the view that in a case of לא ניחה ליה. it is permitted. (7) See Chapter Seven.

21. עיין שו"ע או"ח סימן של"ו סעיף ג'. וע"ע במ"ב סימן שי"ד ס"ק י"א דפסיק רישא אסור אף במלתא דו"בנן 21a. שביעית סימן י"ח ס"ק ו' סימן ט"ס ס"ק ב' ו'ד' וי"ז 22. מועד קטן ג. ועבודה זרה נ: 23. רש"י ע"ז שם ד"ה "אברויי" 24. לפי רש"י מועד קטן ג. ד"ה "סתומי פילי" שכתב דשרי משום דאית ביה פסידה ובע"ז נ: ד"ה "סתומי פילי" כתב   דשרי משום דאוקמי הוא ועיין במשנת יוסף פ"ב מ"ד בשיטות המפרשים ד"ה "ולענין אוקמי אילנא"   25. רש"י ע"ז שם ד"ה "אוקמי" 26. משמעות מרש"י שם ומרמב"ס שביעית פ"ב ד"ה "בית עושה לה צל" עיין משנת יוסף על המשנה ד"ה "וכלל זה"

picking in the normal manner.(8)

The posuk[27] says ״את ספיח קצירך לא תקצור ואת ענבי, נזירך לא תבצור וכו״
"the s'fiach(9) you shall not reap it, and the grapes of your vine...you
shall not pick them". Now[28] this posuk cannot be totally prohibiting
reaping and picking because the Torah permits one to eat produce
which ripens during the Shmittoh year, as it says,[29] ״והיתה שבת
הארץ לכם לאכלה״ meaning that the resting of the fields and the vineyard shall not forbid the produce as far as *eating it* is concerned.
Therefore one is obviously allowed to reap and pick produce.
Rather what the Torah here comes to tell us is that during the
Shmittoh year one must not harvest in the manner that the
harvesters do during the other years but one must make a שינוי
(deviation) in the way he harvests, such as using different
instruments, or processing in a type of location different from the
other six years.(10)

10. Choresh (ploughing)

The prohibition to plough only applies if it is done in a ״שדה״[30]
(field, or open ground). This is defined[31] as being any area of ground
where the earth is suitable for sowing and is not a living area or
ground where people are constantly walking over it. Therefore the
prohibition of choresh does not apply to earthen ground in a house,
courtyard or street.(11)

---

(8) By deviating from the normal manner of reaping, one demonstrates that during
the Shmittoh year the fruit is ownerless.26a
(9) See Chapter Six.
(10) See Chapter Seven.
(11) Choresh in these areas is on Shabbos the melocha of בונה (building), 31a not
prohibited during Shmittoh.

26a. חינוך מצוה שכ״ט 27. ויקרא כה: ה אם פירש״י 28. לפי פיה״מ לר״מ שביעית פ״ח מ״ו וע״ע
תורת כהנים ריש פרשת בהר וירושלמי שביעית פ״ח הל׳ ר׳ 29. ויקרא כה:ו עם פירש״י 30. שבת עג:
31. על פי אגלי טל חורש סימן ט׳ ס״ק ט״ז ד״ה ״ע״כ״ 31a. שבת עג:

11.Use of Machinery

The Chazon Ish[32] explains that if during the Shmittoh year one uses a machine to plough or sow his field then one is still transgressing the principal melocha (Av) which the Torah prohibits. Because even though ploughing which the Torah spoke of was done by the use of oxen and therefore ploughing by way of modern machinery was not what the Torah spoke of, nevertheless it does not make such ploughing a Toldah of choresh, because what classifies an action as a Toldah is only if it is different in action e.g. if one waters seeds then this is not the action of placing seeds in soil therefore it is a Toldah of zore'a. However where one does the same action, placing seeds in the soil, but it is just done by different means, such as by machine instead of by hand, then since doing it with machinery is considered as though *he* is doing the action[12] then sowing with a machine remains an Av.[13]

(12) Therefore it is not considered as him doing an indirect action (גרמא).[32a]

(13) As far as תלש (plucking produce) being considered a Toldah of קצר (reaping produce), and not an Av, this is because the very action of the reaping is different i.e. one is *cutting* the other is *plucking* (see[5*]footnote (75)) whereas sowing by machine or by hand is *placing seeds in holes*.

32.הלכות שבת סימן ל״ו ד״ה ״ולענין״ ולעיל ד״ה ״החורש״ 32a. חזו״א שם

CHAPTER FOUR

TOSEFES SHVIYIS

1. Defining "Tosefes Shviyis"

In addition to the prohibition of melocha on the land and trees during Shmittoh, there was originally a prohibition of melocha[1] sometime before the Shmittoh year commenced.[1*] This is referred to as Tosefes Shviyis[2] (lit. addition to Shviyis)—which is a thirty day period. This prohibition became nullified, and therefore it should mean that nowadays one may do all melocha on the land and trees right up until Rosh Hashona, when the Shmittoh year begins.[2a] However for other reasons one may not do various melochos[3] within forty-four days of Shmittoh.[4][4,5*]

According to Rabbi Akiva Tosefes Shviyis is derived from the posuk[1] "בחריש ובקציר תשבות".[1*] According to Rabbi Yishmoel, it is an oral tradition that Moshe received at Sinai, our not having been given a basis for it in the Written Law (הלכה למשה מסיני).[1*]

A decree was made by Bais Shammai and Bais Hillel during the period of the Second Bais haMikdosh that ploughing is forbidden even before this thirty day period.[2*]

This extension was from Pesach in a grain field and from Shavous in an orchard.[6*] This decree was made in order to prevent one from becoming confused and possibly ploughing during the Shmittoh year itself.[2*]

(1) Which melochos are prohibited is a dispute amongst the Rishonim.[1*]
(2) This is the pronunciation used in the Bavli. The Yerushalmi[1a] refers to it as Tosfos Shviyis.
(2a) See "Shmittoh in Depth" Chapter One no. 1
(3) These are sowing fruit tree seeds, planting fruit saplings and, in some instances grafting onto fruit trees or lavering.[4,5*]
(4) Although from ט"ז אב (inclusive) until כ"ט אלול totals forty-four days, some poskim allow this melocha to be done during the day of ט"ז אב providing one stops some time before the end of this day, because on account of the rule מקצת היום ככולו (part of a day is like a whole day[1b]) it can be considered as having not done melocha the whole day of ט"ז באב. Consequently י"ז אב marks the first full day when this prohibition would apply. This is the p'sak of the Rosh[1c] and the Chazon Ish.[1d]

1a. כלאים פ"ח הל' א' 1b. פסחים ד. ועוד מקומות 1c. הלכות ערלה סימן ט' 1d.שביעית סימן י"ז
סוף ס"ק כ"ט 1. שמות לד: כא

2. The rule for Tosefes Shviyis is laid down as follows:[2]

1) Even if a melocha is forbidden midorysa during Shmittoh, (i.e. Avos[(5)]) it is permitted to be done even during the last thirty day period of Tosefes Shviyis providing that it will only benefit the produce of the sixth year.[(6)] However, if the melocha will only benefit the growth of a tree or stem of a plant and not the actual produce of the sixth year, then it is forbidden to do such melocha during the last thirty day period of Tosefes Shviyis. Concerning ploughing[(7)] it is forbidden miderabbonon, either from Pesach or from Shavuos[3] depending on whether it is an orchard or grain field.[2*]

2) If a melocha is only forbidden miderabbonon during Shmittoh, (i.e. Toldos[4(8)]) then even if it will only benefit a tree or stem and not its produce it is permitted during the whole period of Tosefes Shviyis. This is because being that the melochos are forbidden miderabbonon, then the Rabbonon themselves have the option not to extend their prohibition to the period of Tosefes Shviyis.

3. The Nullification of Tosefes Shviyis

After the destruction of the Second Bais haMikdosh the decree of Bais Shammai and Bais Hillel continued until Rabbon Gamliel and his Bais Din took conference about these two extended times of Tosefes Shviyis because they saw that in keeping this the land was becoming ruined.[5(9)] Therefore they nullified this Tosefes Shviyis

(5) See Chapter Three.

(6) Being *melocha of the sixth year* it is understood that this does not come within the Torah prohibition of Tosefes Shviyis. The factor of confusion is relevant only to the decree of Bais Shammai and Bais Hillel, not here.

(7) Ploughing improves existing growth i.e. helps thicken the bark of trees, but does not necessarily improve its produce.[2a]

(8) See Chapter Three.

(9) Seemingly a bigger problem than people coming to confusion and ploughing during Shmittoh.

2. לפי הר״ש שביעית פ״ב מ״ב ד״ה "מעדרין" 2a. ירושלמי שביעית פ״א הל׳ א׳ 3. רע״ק שביעית אות י״א 4. חזו״א שביעית סימן י״ז ס״ק י״ח 5. תוס׳ מועד קטן ג. ד״ה "כל" ועיין בתפארת ישראל פ״א אות ג׳

allowing melocha to be done up until Rosh Hashona of the
Shmittoh year.[3*]

4. After the Nullification until Nowadays

After the nullification of the halocha of Tosefes Shviyis it became
permitted to do even melochos forbidden midorysa as normal until
Rosh Hashona of the Shmittoh year. However, even nowadays
there is a halocha that one may not do certain melochos with fruit
trees beginning forty-four days before Shmittoh.[4,5*]

CHAPTER FIVE

DETERMINING TO WHICH YEAR A CROP BELONGS

(חנטה,הבאת שליש, לקיטה, השרשה, גמר פרי)

1. חנטה

All fruit, except for grapes and olives, which have their חנטה [2*] (to be explained) during Shmittoh are considered "Peiros Shviyis" (fruit of the Seventh year) and have *Kedushas Shviyis* (sanctity of the seventh year).[1*] Fruit which had their חנטה in the sixth year and are still growing when Shmittoh begins are considered produce of the sixth year and have no *Kedushas Shviyis*.[1] When is this stage reached? It would be helpful to trace the development of a fruit.

What first grows out of the twig of a tree is a green oblong formation referred to as the "bud". This is usually made up of green petals which are bunched up together:

These green petals eventually open up and then what is called the "blossom" appears.

What forms in the middle of this flower and appears as extending from the stem is what is referred to as the "pistil".

1. רמב״ם שמיטה ויובל פ״ד הל׳ ט׳

The fruit eventually begins to form at the bottom of the pistil:

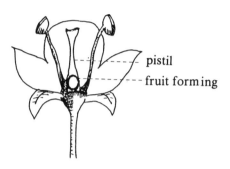

pistil

fruit forming

The fruit at this stage is like a small hard ball inside the bottom of the pistil. This fruit formation begins to expand in size and pushes out the sides of the pistil so that the bottom of the pistil eventually appears thicker than the stem below it so that the pistil no longer looks like a continuation of the stem:

This stage is referred to as the stage of חנטה i.e. when the formation of the fruit appears blossoming out.[2]

---

2. עיין מלאכת שלמה שביעית פ״ד מ״י ד״ה ״משיוציאו״ וז״ל ״דהוצאות פרי קרוי׳ חנטה בלשון רבותינו״

2. הבאת שליש

Grain, some legumes, grapes and olives which complete the first third of their ripeness (הבאת שליש)[2*] during Shmittoh are considered as Peiros Shviyis and have *Kedushas Shviyis.*[1*] Grain and legumes will have an issur S'fichim3 (see Chapter Six). If they reach this stage during the sixth year then even if they grow into the Shmittoh year they are still considered sixth year produce and have no *Kedushas Shviyis.*4 Grain and legumes will have no issur S'fichim.

3. לקיטה

Vegetables (ירקות) which are picked (לקיטה)[2*] during the Shmittoh year are considered Peiros Shviyis.[1*]

4. השרשה

Legumes such as rice, kinds of millet and sesame which take root (השרשה)[2*] during the Shmittoh year are considered Peiros Shviyis.[1*] There is however an opinion that concerning these species, only when they have their גמר פרי (explained next) during Shmittoh are they considered Peiros Shviyis. [1*] If they reach גמר פרי during the sixth year they are sixth year produce and have no *Kedushas Shviyis.*5

5. גמר פרי

The term לקיטה is interchangeable with גמר פרי (the full maturation of the produce) because לקיטה is done immediately following the גמר פרי.6

---

3. רמב״ם שם הל׳ י׳ 4. רמב״ם שם הל׳ ט׳ 5. רמב״ם שם הל׳ י״א 6. תוס׳ ראש השנה יג : ד״ה ״אחר״

CHAPTER SIX

ספיחים (S'FICHIM)

1. Defining "S'fichim"

Seeds which fell from produce during harvesting and took root themselves, or produce which grew from roots left in the ground after the last harvest[1] are both examples of S'fichim.[1][2] Wild herbs or vegetables are also examples of S'fichim.[2]

Tree fruit are a form of S'fichim since they grow by themselves.[3][2*]

2. Issur S'fichim

A distinction must be drawn between the term "S'fichim" which refers to all spontaneous growth and *"issur S'fichim"* which refers to that spontaneous growth which has a particular prohibition (to be explained).

The general rule is that crops that could be intentionally sown and claimed to be S'fichim are prohibited, such as vegetables, grains and legumes,[3] while trees being that they do not bear fruit for some time, are a form of permitted S'fichim, since people are not suspected of sowing them during Shmittoh.

---

(1) Even though the original roots were sown intentionally nevertheless this second time the growth was spontaneous.
(2) "S'fiach" (ספיח) in the singular.
(3) Even though the tree was originally planted intentionally. See footnote (1).

1. עיין רמב״ם שמיטה ויובל פ״ד הל׳ א׳   2. רמב״ם שם ״ה עשבים והירקות שעלו מאיליהן ואין להן זרע״ (היינו שנזרעו בלי עבודת אדם) 3. רמב״ם שם הל׳ ג׳

3. Issur S'fichim—Midorysa or Miderabbonon

There is a dispute between Rabbi Akiva and the Rabbonon as to whether issur S'fichim is prohibited midorysa or miderabbonon.[1*] Rabbi Akiva says it is midorysa and the Rabbonon say it is miderabbonon. The Chazon Ish[4] rules that issur S'fichim is miderabbonon, and is prohibited not only to be eaten, but no benefit may be derived from it.[5(4)]

---

(4) Except for grain to be used as a meal offering in the Mikdosh such as the Omer, since the benefit forbidden is personal benefit (איסור גברא).[5a]

---

4. שביעית סימן ט׳ ס״ק י״ז 5. חזו״א בסדר השביעית סעיף א׳ ״ואף ליתן לבהמה אסור״ ובסימן י״ג ס״ק ט״ז ד״ה ״ויש״ 5a. חזו״א שביעית שם

CHAPTER SEVEN

GUARDED (משומר) AND WORKED (ונעבד) PRODUCE

1. Defining "משומר"

"משומר" refers to where public access has been denied to Shmittoh produce which should have been left ownerless.(הפקר, Chapter Five [1*]) The basic questions which surround the subject of משומר are

(1) Does it remain forbidden to be eaten, even should later the owner relinquish his rights?[1*]

(2) Is it forbidden merely to reap it in the normal way, but should it be reaped with a שינוי, deviation, it is permitted?[1*]

2. Defining "נעבד"

"נעבד" refers to Shmittoh produce which grew with the help of forbidden melocha.[2*]

The Halocha Today
משומר

The Rambam nowhere mentions that the consumption of משומר produce is forbidden. Several Achronim[1] assume from this that his view is that the consumption of משומר produce is permitted.

The Chazon Ish's view on this subject is unclear. In one place[2] he writes that esrogim which are from משומר are permitted. Some[3] write that the intention of the Chazon Ish is to permit משומר only in an emergency situation. In another place[4] he writes that משומר produce is forbidden.

1. הר״י קרקוס ד, (כ״ב כ״ד — ח׳, י׳) הכפות תמרים סוכה ל״ט ב׳: וערוך השלחן העתיד סי׳ כ״א ס״ק ו׳. 2. שביעית סימן י׳ ס״ק ו׳. 3. הרב בנימין זילבר הלכות שביעית חלק א׳ מלואים עמוד קפ״א. 4. בסוף הלכות שביעית בסדר השביעית ס״א.

Many of his Talmidim claim that he permitted משומר produce. The general custom in B'nei Brak is to permit the eating of fruit which was משומר. The custom, however, in Yerushalayim is to consider their consumption forbidden.

נעבד

Some[5] write that they heard that the Chazon Ish gave the P'sak that the consumption of משומר produce and *even* נעבד produce is permitted, providing one eats it with *Kedushas Shviyis.* So is the custom of his followers.[6]

The custom in Yerushalayim is to forbid the consumption of נעבד produce.

———————————————

Subject matter such as the prohibition of doing business with Shmittoh produce, how to treat it and biyur (removal of Shmittoh produce) since they involve much practical halochic implications, are discussed in the section "Halochos of Shmittoh".

5 שו״ת חשב האפוד סי׳ כ״ב. 6 ע׳ משנת יוסף חלק ג׳ עמוד קמ״ט.

SHMITTOH

IN

DEPTH

CHAPTER ONE

SHMITTOH AND YOVEL

1. Shmittoh begins the first of Tishrei

The Mishna[1] tells us that the Shmittoh year commences from the first day of the month of Tishrei (Rosh Hashona). The Gemora[2] derives this from the following:

The Torah[3] says ...מקרא קדש יהיה לכם...ובחודש השביעי באחד לחודש״ ״יום תרועה יהיה לכם״ "The first day of the seventh month (1st of Tishrei)...shall be a holy day(Yom Tov) to you...a day to you of blowing the horn (Shofar)". Nowhere in this posuk does it state that it is a *Yom Din* (day of judgement). From where do we know that the 1st of Tishrei is a day of judgement?

The Gemora derives this from two p'sukim in Tehillim:[4] ״תקעו בחודש שופר, בכסה ליום חגנו״ "blow shofar at the time of the New Moon on the Chag *(Yom Tov)* when the moon is covered (i.e. hidden from our sight)". Which *Yom Tov* do we have when it is a day that the moon is covered, i.e. a new moon? It is Rosh Hashona, the 1st of Tishrei.

The next posuk goes on to state ״כי חק לישראל הוא משפט לאלקי יעקב״ "for it is an ordinance to Yisroel, it is a day of judgement for the G-d of Ya'akov".

We know from the above that the 1st of Tishrei is the day on which we are judged. The Torah[5] says elsewhere ״מרשית השנה ועד אחרית השנה״ "from the beginning of the year until the end of the year" and the Gemora explains this posuk to mean that at the beginning of the year there is a judgement in that it is decided by HaShem what will be up to the end of it, therefore ״מרשית השנה״ refers to the 1st of Tishrei.

By way of *gezera shova* of the word ״שנה״ in the posuk here ״מרשית״

1. ראש השנה פ״א מ״א 2.ראש השנה ח.־ ח : 3. במדבר כט :א 4. פא : ה׳ /וה׳ 5. דברים יא :יב

"השנה" and the word "שנה" in the posuk concerning Shmittoh "ובשנה השביעית שבת שבתון יהיה לארץ" we learn that just as "מרשית השנה" refers to the 1st of Tishrei so also "ובשנה השביעית" refers to the year of Shmittoh as beginning on the 1st of Tishrei.

2. The entry into Eretz Yisroel and beginning to count the Shmittoh cycle

The letter "ה"[6] of the word "הארץ"[7] ("*the* land") and the words "אשר אני נותן לכם" ("which I give you") were explicitly stated in order to inform the Am Yisroel that the count of the Shmittoh Cycle was to begin only when they entered Eretz Yisroel and not upon entering any other vicinity which they might inhabit.[8]

This means[9] that had the Torah written "כי תבואו אל ארץ אשר יהיה לכם" "when you come into a land which will belong to you" then it could well have been assumed that they were to begin counting the Shmittoh Cycle even before they came into Eretz Yisroel,[10] when they would enter Ever Hayarden,[(1)] this being the first area that the Am Yisroel were to reach which would eventually belong to them. It was to be the inheritance of the tribes Reuven and Gad[11] and half of the tribe of Menashe.[12]

However, such an assumption is ruled out by the fact that the Torah here does not simply say "ארץ" "*a* land", but rather speaks of "הארץ" with a "ה", therefore describing that it is "*the* land", that land which is in some way more special than any other land. It must have the unique quality of being זבת חלב ודבש,[13(2)] clearly excluding the area of Ever Hayarden,[14] where the land is not of such quality.

(1) Ever Hayarden lit. "across the Jordan (river)". This was the name given to the area of land on the eastern side of the Jordan river. Before the Am Yisroel reached this vicinity it was occupied by the Kings סיחון and עוג.[10a]
(2) Its quality is such that it causes the goats living on it to have milk flowing from them and the dates growing from it to have honey flowing from them.[13a]

6. לפי המלבי״ם 7. ויקרא כה :ב. 8. לפי תורת כהנים ריש פרשת בהר 9. תורת כהנים שם 10. חפץ חיים על ת״כ שם 10a. דברים ג:ח 11. דברים ג: יב ועיין פירש״י 12. דברים ג: יג 13. חפץ חיים שם 13a. רש״י שמות יג :ה 14. חפץ חיים שם

There is however one section of Ever Hayarden, Cheshbon and its environs, where the land is of such quality.[15(3)] The assumption would now be that they were to begin counting the Shmittoh Cycle when they entered this vicinity.

Such an assumption is ruled out, since the posuk goes on to say "אשר אני נותן לכם" "which I *give* you", informing us that the obligation to count the Shmittoh Cycle was only to begin when they were to enter the area of land which Hashem had promised to *give us*[16] referring to the area beyond Ever Hayarden, on the western side of the Jordan river, but not that area which was captured by them and which they themselves desired to live in, but was not included in Hashem's promise.[17(4)] The counting of the Shmittoh Cycle however did not commence until fourteen years after entry into the Land (see "Shmittoh in General" no.4)

3. How the Yovel Cycle is counted—Rabbi Yehudah and the Rabbonon[18]

One way of fixing the date for Yovel is after completion of seven Shmittoh Cycles, Yovel being the fiftieth year with the next Shmittoh Cycle beginning the following year.[(5)] If so, each Yovel Cycle consists of fifty years. This is the view of the Rabbonon. Rabbi Yehudah, however, says that the new Yovel year, the fiftieth year from the previous Yovel, also marks the first year of the next

(3) One will notice that the Toras Kohanim here refers to Cheshbon as עמן ומואב. This is because although when the Am Yisroel reached this vicinity it was occupied by סיחון nevertheless it had been previously ruled by מואב,[15a] therefore חשבון is sometimes referred to as "עמן ומואב".

(4) Later on, after the division of the land when the Am Yisroel became obligated to observe Shmittoh, this obligation extended also to those tribes living in Ever Hayarden.[17a]

(5) In such a case it is termed "שנת חמישים אינה מן המנין" i.e. the fiftieth year is not included in the count of the following cycle.

15. ר"ש משאנץ וראב"ד על ת"כ שם 15a. במדבר כא: כו וע" פירש"י 16. בראשית יב: ז 17. לפי ר"ש משאנץ וראב"ד שם 17a. ר"ש משאנץ שם 18. ראש השנה ט.

Shmittoh Cycle,[6] meaning each Yovel Cycle consists of only forty-nine years,[19] the first Shmittoh of the new Yovel Cycle occurring only *six* years after Yovel. There is a difference of opinion amongst the Rishonim as to which one of these two views is the halocha.[20]

4. Conditions for the observance of Yovel

The Torah[21] says "וקדשתם את שנת החמישים שנה וקראתם דרור בארץ לכל יושביה יובל היא תהיה לכם וכו'" ''and you shall sanctify the fiftieth year and proclaim freedom in the land to all its inhabitants, it shall be a Yovel to you etc''. Two conditions for the obligation to observe Yovel are derived from the words "כל יושביה", ''all its inhabitants'':[22]

1) By the fact that the posuk mentions "*all* its inhabitants''. This tells us that there is only an obligation to observe the Yovel year if *all* of the Am Yisroel are dwelling in Eretz Yisroel and Ever Hayarden[7] and not at a time when *any* of them are in exile.[8]

(6) In such a case it is termed "שנת חמישים עולה לכאן ולכאן" i.e. the fiftieth year is the Yovel and it begins the next Yovel Cycle.[18a]

(7) See footnote (1). Regarding the rule of רובו ככולו (most is like *all*)[22a] it clearly appears from the text of the Toras Kohanim[22b] and: ערכין לב and Rambam[22c] that this rule has not been applied here since they say "after the tribes Reuven, Gad, and half of Menashe were exiled the Yovel became nullified" even though the other ten tribes (a *majority* of Am Yisroel) were not yet exiled. Also the rule of רובו ככולו does not apply in a case where the Torah precisely denotes "all".[22d] There is also an understanding[22e] that רובו ככולו means רוב מתוך כולו, that in considering the רוב it must be a majority of a still-existing totality. Some Jews residing outside of Eretz Yisroel for business purposes, etc. would not detract from all Jews being considered as living in Eretz Yisroel (as seen concerning זבולון). Such residence not being considered a form of exile.

(8) There is a difference of opinion amongst the Rishonim.[22f] Rashi understands the Torah here in saying "all" means literally that everyone must be living in Eretz Yisroel and Ever Hayarden, each tribe in its own area, Tosfos understands that by "all" the Torah means *''all of the twelve tribes''*, i.e. that it is sufficient to have just *some* representatives of each of the twelve tribes living there, even though most of each tribe may not be living in Eretz Yisroel and Ever Hayarden. Even according to Rashi if there are at least some representatives of each tribe living there then the Yovel must be kept miderabbonon.

18a. רש"י ערכין יב: ד"ה "שנת חמישים עולה" 19. רש"י שם 20. עיין רמב"ם שמיטה ויובל פ"י הל' ז' שפסק כרבנן עיין רדב"ז שם אבל תוס' ר"ה ט. ד"ה "ולאפוקי" ובע"ז ט: ד"ה "האי" פסקו כרבי יהודה. 21. ויקרא כה: י 22. ערכין לב: וירושלמי שביעית פ"י הל' ב' 22a. ע" נזיר מב. 22b. בהר פ"ב ג' 22c. שמיטה ויובל פ"י הל' ח' 22d. הגהות מהרצ"ב רנשבורג נזיר מב. 22e. שו"ת חתם סופר או"ח סימן ק"מ 22f. רש"י ותוס' ע" תוס' גיטין לו. ד"ה "בזמן"

2) That the posuk mentions "יושביה", "its inhabitants", tells us that Eretz Yisroel must be inhabited in the manner designated at the time of the חלוקת הארץ ("Division of the Land," See "Shmittoh in General" no. 4), that is, each tribe[9] inhabiting their own area of land and not that they are living in a mixed fashion, such as the tribe of Binyomin inhabiting the area assigned to the tribe of Yehudah, or visa versa.

5. The connection between the mitzvoh of Yovel and the mitzvoh of Shmittoh

Rebbi[10] explains[23] that during a time when there can be no mitzvoh of observing the Yovel year there is also no mitzvoh midorysa of observing the Shmittoh year. Rebbi derives this from the fact that the Torah[24] says "וזה דבר השמיטה שמוט וגו'". The Torah here doubles its wording ("שמיטה שמוט"), and from this extra wording[25] Rebbi derives that this speaks of the two instances of Shmittoh, the seventh year and the Yovel year. The Shmittoh and Yovel year are here mentioned in juxtaposition, and by way of *hekesh* (comparison of subjects in juxtaposition) we derive that only when there is an obligation midorysa to observe the Yovel year is there an obligation midorysa to observe the Shmittoh year. Accordingly, during a period when there is no obligation midorysa to observe the Yovel year then midorysa there is also no obligation to observe the Shmittoh year. An obligation miderabbonon does exist, however, and the tribes of Yehudah and Binyomin continued to observe (according to Rebbi) Shmittoh miderabbonon even after the exile of the ten tribes. The Rabbonon,[26] however, disagree

(9) Whether the entire tribe, or just some representatives of each tribe, see footnote (8).
(10) Rebbi Yehudah haNassi, known also as "Rabbeinu haKodosh".

23. ירושלמי שם 24. דברים טו: ב 25. על פי פני משה שם 26. ירושלמי שם

with Rebbi and are of the opinion that even when there is no obligation midorysa to observe the Yovel year nevertheless there is still an obligation midorysa to observe the Shmittoh year. The Rabbonon derive[27] this from that which the Torah[28] says ״וספרת לך שבע שבתות שנים שבע שנים שבע פעמים והיו לך ימי שבע שבתות השנים תשע וארבעים שנה״ ''and you shall count for yourself seven Shmittoh years, seven times seven years, and they shall be for you, these seven Shmittoh years, forty nine years''. What the Torah wishes to tell us by adding the words "and they shall be for you, these seven Shmittoh years" is that you shall be obligated in observing these seven Shmittoh years even though there will be no Yovel year following them.[29(11)]

According to this view it follows that even after the exile of the ten tribes there was an obligation midorysa for the tribes of Yehudah and Binyomin to observe the Shmittoh year.[30]

---

(11) "They shall be for you" meaning they shall *continue* to be for you.

---

27. תורת כהנים פרשת בהר פרשתא ב׳ הובא בתוס׳ ערכין לב: ד״ה ״מנו״ ועי׳ רש״י גיטין לו. ד״ה ״בשביעית בזמן הזה״ 28. ויקרא כה:ח 29. על פי חפץ חיים על ת״כ שם 30. ר״ש משאנץ וראב״ד על ת״כ שם

CHAPTER TWO

SHMITTOH THROUGH THE AGES

1. The permanence of קדושה ראשונה

קדושה ראשונה קידשה לשעתה וקידשה לעתיד לבא

The Gemora poses the question as to whether the *Kedusha Rishona* was such that it could not become nullified, or under certain circumstances could become nullified. In some places[1] this question is posed with regard to the *Kedusha Rishona* of ירושלים והבית and in other places[2] this question is asked with regard to the *Kedusha Rishona* of the Land. It is Rabbi Yossi[3] who concludes that it was a kedusha which could become nullified. The Gemora[4] suggests that this view is based upon a particular posuk in Sefer Nechemya:

In reference to the time following the rebuilding of the Bais haMikdosh, when Ezra haSofer came from Bovel to Yerushalayim with people from the exile, the posuk[5] says מן השבים הקהל כל ויעשו״ השבי סכות וישבו בסכות כי לא עשו מימי ישוע בן נון כן בני ישראל עד היום ההוא מאד״ גדולה שמחה ותהי "and all the congregation of those who had come back out of captivity constructed succos (boothes for Chag HaSuccos) and dwelt in the succos, for since the days of Yehoshua bin Nun until that day they (the Am Yisroel) had not done so, and there was great rejoicing". Rabbi Yossi understands[6] that the words "they (the Am Yisroel) had not done so" does *not* refer to what the posuk said in the beginning, regarding constructing succos, but means to say that since the days of Yehoshua bin Nun to that day the Am Yisroel *had not established a kedusha to Eretz Yisroel.* In other words Ezra had now established a kedusha in Eretz Yisroel, the last time such a kedusha was established having been in the time of Yehoshua. Therefore we infer from this posuk that since the

---

1. כגון שבועות טז. 2. כגון חולין ז. 3. עי׳ ערכין לב: 4. ערכין שם 5. נחמיה ח: יז 6. לפי פירש״י שם בגמ׳ ד״ה ״אלא מקיש ביאתם בימי עזרא וגו׳״

Kedusha Rishona established by Yehoshua had become nullified, Ezra haSofer needed to re-establish the kedusha for a second time. Obviously the *Kedusha Rishona* had only been temporary.[1]

This clearly poses a question on the opinion that the *Kedusha Rishona* was established to exist permanently. The Gemora answers that this opinion understands the words "for since the days of Yehoshua bin Nun to that day they (the Am Yisroel) had not done so" do in fact refer back to the subject of succos and are not speaking of establishing a kedusha for the Land. What is meant, however, by "succos" is not literally "boothes" as may have been assumed, but means "protection".[2] That is, Ezra implored Hashem to nullify the inclination of the Am Yisroel towards idolatry and this created a 'protection' for them, something which had not been asked for by Yehoshua.

2. The kedusha of Eretz Yisroel and the kedusha of ירושלים והבית

Tosfos and Rambam

The Gemora[7] poses the question of the nullifiability of *Kedusha Rishona* both with regard to the Land and with regard to ירושלים והבית. Tosfos[8] and the Rambam[9] distinguish, in their p'sak, between the *Kedusha Rishona* of the Land and the *Kedusha Rishona* of ירושלים והבית. The Geonim[10] however, pasken that the *Kedusha Rishona* of both the Land and ירושלים והבית were the same.

Tosfos rejected the approach of the Geonim, since this would create a problem with two statements of the Amora Rabbi Yochanan. Concerning קדושת הארץ Rabbi Yochanan says[11] that it

---

(1) See below no. 2 for the explanation of the Rambam as to why the *Kedusha Rishona* should only have been of a temporary nature.

(2) As we find "סכותה לראשי ביום נשק"[6a] "You *protected* my head in the day of battle."

6a. תהלים קמ:ח 7. שבועות טז. חולין ז. ועוד מקומות. 8. יבמות פב: ד"ה "ירושה" 9. בית הבחירה פ"ו הל' ט"ז 10. עי' רמב"ם שמיטה ויובל פ"י הל' ה' 11. יבמות שם

was a temporary kedusha (קידשה לשעתה), yet concerning the *Kedusha Rishona* of ירושלים והבית he says[12] it is permanent (קידשה לשעתה וקידשה לעתיד לבוא.) Obviously, unlike the Geonim, there is a difference between the two areas of kedusha. Why the difference? This will be clarified as we go on.

קדושת הארץ

According to the Rambam[13] the *Kedusha Rishona* of the Land was created because Eretz Yisroel had been conquered. When the Gemora poses its question as to whether this *Kedusha Rishona* was temporary (קידשה לשעתה) or permanent (קידשה לעתיד לבא) the question is:

a) whether this conquest created the kedusha and is thereafter also required to maintain it, meaning that should ever the conquest cease to exist then the kedusha would also be nullified, or

b) the conquest was merely a means of bringing the kedusha into existence but is not required to prolong it, meaning that if Jewish sovereignty ceased to exist the kedusha would still continue. The Rambam himself takes the former view.

קדושת ירושלים והבית

The Rambam[14] says that the *Kedusha Rishona* of ירושלים והבית was created because of the presence of the Shechina having come to dwell there, and when the Gemora poses its question of whether the *Kedusha Rishona* was a temporary kedusha or is permanently existing, the question is:

a) whether this *Kedusha Rishona* was established to exist only for as long as the "מחיצות"[15] (walls) around Yerushalayim would remain standing, but not if they are destroyed,[(3)] or

b) whether this *Kedusha Rishona* was established to exist in spite of the fact that there would no longer be walls, the kedusha being

---

(3) Even though the presence of the Shechina would not become removed by this, because even after these places have become desolate the Torah[15a] refers to them as "מקדשכם" "your places of kedusha".

dependent solely on the presence of the Shechina which, having been brought by the construction of the walls, would always remain. The Rambam himself takes this latter view.[4]

It is therefore possible for קדושת הארץ to be contingent on the presence of the Am Yisroel while קדושת ירושלים והבית can be permanent. According to Rabbi Yochanon, with regard to קדושת הארץ option "a" would be correct and with regard to קדושת ירושלים והבית option "b" would be correct.

The Geonim

The Geonim[16] remained with the original assumption of Tosfos, that the *Kedusha Rishona* of ירושלים והבית has the same essential permanence as the *Kedusha Rishona* of the Land[17] meaning that whatever permanence the *Kedusha Rishona* of the Land had, the קדושת ירושלים והבית would have the same degree of permanence.[5]

It follows that according to the Geonim the question as to whether the *Kedusha Rishona* was a temporary kedusha or is permanent can be suggested to be:

a) whether the people establishing the *Kedusha Rishona* in both areas only had the power to establish it for as long as the very circumstances under which it was established would remain but for no longer, or

(4) Concerning this, the Tosfos differ with the Rambam and learn that the *Kedusha Rishona* of ירושלים והבית was created only by the walls (of Yerushalayim) and has nothing to do with the presence of the Shechina which dwells there. Therefore when the Talmud poses its question as to whether this kedusha was nullifiable or is permanently existing the question is: a) whether the walls created the kedusha and are thereafter also required to prolong it, meaning that if ever the walls would cease to stand then the kedusha would become nullified, thus it was nullifiable kedusha, or b) whether the walls were merely a means of bringing the kedusha into existence but are not required to prolong it, meaning that if ever the walls were destroyed the kedusha would still continue to exist, the kedusha being of a permanent nature.
(5) As to the question of the Tosfos posed by such an assumption, that Rabbi Yochanan seems to contradict himself, this remains a problem according to the view of the Geonim.

16. רמב״ם שמיטה ויובל פ״י הל׳ ה׳ 17. לפי כסף משנה שם בגלל שהוא מעורב קדושת הבית בתוך שיטת הגאונים שאמרו שקדושה ראשונה בשאר א״י קדשה לשעתה וקדשה לעתיד לבא.

b) whether they had the power to establish it even for a time when these circumstances would no longer be there. The Geonim themselves take this latter view.

In summation, the Geonim and the Rambam agree that the kedusha of ירושלים והבית was permanent and not contingent on the continued existence of the walls which brought it about. They disagree, however, whether there was a need for the continued sovereignty over Eretz Yisroel, brought about by Yehoshua's conquest, in order to maintain קדושת הארץ.

3. The number of Shmittoh and Yovel years until חורבן בית ראשון

The Rambam[18] states that according to the view of Rabbi Yehudah[19] the Yovel year is counted as part of the Shmittoh Cycle which follows it.[(6)]   This would mean that from the time that Yehoshua and the Am Yisroel entered Eretz Yisroel (10th Nisson 2488) until the destruction of the First Bais haMikdosh 9th Av 3338 the Am Yisroel observed 17 Yovel years. The Rambam calculates this as follows: The period between the entry into Eretz Yisroel until the Destruction was 850 years.[20] The number of Yovel years within this period according to Rabbi Yehudah is calculated by dividing it by 49 which gives the total of 17 Yovel years with a remainder of 17 years. Since however they only started to count the Shmittoh Cycle 14 years after their entry into Eretz Yisroel (See "Shmittoh in General" Chapter One numbers 3,4) therefore in subtracting 14 from the above figure we are left with a total of 17 Yovel years with a remainder of 3 years. Thus according to Rabbi Yehudah the Destruction was in the third year of the Yovel Cycle.

According to the view of the Rabbonon,[21] from the time that Yehoshua and the Am Yisroel entered Eretz Yisroel until the Destruction, the Am Yisroel observed 16 Yovel years with a

(6) See Chapter One.[3*]

18. שמיטה ויובל פ״י הל׳ ג׳ 19. עיין ראב״ד שם 20. מתוך דבריו בחשבונו אחר זה 21. עיין ראב״ד שם

remainder of 36 years. That is, the amount of Yovel years within the period of 850 years is calculated by dividing it by 50, which gives the total of exactly 17 Yovel years. However, they only started the count of the Shmittoh Cycle 14 years after their entry into Eretz Yisroel, therefore in subtracting 14 from the last figure we are left with the total of 16 Yovel years with a remainder of 36 years. According to this, the Destruction took place in the 36th year of a Yovel Cycle, meaning that it was in a year following Shmittoh, and being at the end of 850 years after the entry into Eretz Yisroel, this therefore brings us to the year 3338.[22]

4. Ezra haSofer and the renewal of קדושת הארץ

As far as the *Kedusha Rishona* of ירושלים והבית is concerned then according to both the Rishonim and the Geonim (see above, no. 2) this kedusha did not become nullified. This, however raises the following problem.

There is a section of Sefer Nechemya[23] which clearly shows that when Ezra haSofer came from Bovel with the people of the exile he conducted a special ceremony in the Bais haMikdosh conforming with the details of how a kedusha is to be established there. Why should this be necessary if the kedusha never became nullified in ירושלים והבית? The Gemora[24] answers that what Ezra did was merely a reminder that there was an already existing kedusha there.

According to the opinion of the Geonim[25] the *Kedusha Rishona* of the Land was also established by means that it would exist permanently, meaning that even after the First Destruction, those people of the Am Yisroel who remained living in Eretz Yisroel[26] observed the mitzvoh of the Shmittoh year. However it is questionable if they observed it as an obligation midorysa or miderabbonon, depending on the view of Rebbi or the Rabbonon.[7]

(7) See Chapter One.[5*]

22. מלכים ב' כה:ח 23. נחמיה יב 24. שבועות טז. ועיין ברמב"ם בית הבחירה פ"ו הל' יד ועי' בכסף משנה שמיטה ויובל פ"י הל' ה' 25. הובא ברמב"ם שמיטה ויובל פ"י הל' ה' 26. עיין ירמיה נב: טו

5. Counting the Shmittoh Cycle after the חורבן בית ראשון

According to the view of the Geonim that after the First Destruction the count of the Shmittoh Cycles never stopped, it means that the Shmittoh year was not year 3415 (see "Shmittoh in General", Chapter Two no. 4). That is, being that the Destruction took place on a Motzoai Shmittoh,[27] and it was seventy-seven years later when the *Kedusha Shniya* was established and the count of the cycle started again (ibid), therefore accordingly the Shmittoh year was actually this seventy-seventh year. In other words, in the opinion of the Geonim, according to Rebbi[8] the count after the First Destruction was an obligation miderabbonon and so it continued as an obligation miderabbonon after the building of the Second Bais haMikdosh. In the opinion of the Geonim according to the Rabbonon[9] the count after the First Destruction was an obligation midorysa and so it continued as an obligation midorysa after the building of the Second Bais haMikdosh.

6. מנו יובלות לקדש שמיטין

After Ezra's establishment of the *Kedusha Shniya* the observance of the Shmittoh was resumed.[10] The Gemora[28] says that those who were living in Eretz Yisroel in the time of Ezra observed Yovel[29] as well as Shmittoh. Since, after the exile of the ten tribes, only Yehudah and Binyomin remained, the requirement of כל יושביה[11] was no longer present. It was Yehudah and Binyomin who were exiled to Bovel at the time of the First Destruction and it was they who returned with Ezra to Eretz Yisroel.[12]

---

(8) See ibid.
(9) See ibid.
(10) It is questionable if it was observed midorysa or miderabbonon (see ibid).
(11) See Chapter One.[4*]
(12) According to Tosfos[29a] the Gemora at this point does not realize that Yirmiyohu had brought back representatives of each tribe. Tosfos is left with the question as to how this could be if we see in Sefer Ezra that there were these representatives.

27. רמב״ם שם הל׳ ג׳. 28. ערכין לב: 29. אף ביאתן בימי עזרא מנו שמיטין ויובלות 29a. גיטין לו. ד״ה ״בזמן״

Why, then, did they observe Yovel? Rabbi Nachman bar Yitzchok[13] answers "מנו יובלות לקדש שמיטין" "they (the tribes of Yehudah and Binyomin after the exile of the ten tribes[14]) did not *observe* the Yovel years but nevertheless they *counted* the Yovel years in order to keep a correct counting so as to sanctify the Shmittoh years at their appropriate time." The Gemora assumes that this favours the view of the Rabbonon[30] that the Yovel year is אינו מן המנין[15] and this is in fact how the Gemora concludes.[31] This clearly indicates that it continued to be counted midorysa even if it was not being observed. The Gemora then proves from various p'sukim that in fact Yirmiyohu had at some stage brought back to Eretz Yisroel some representatives from each of the ten tribes so that they did not merely count the fiftieth year but they actually began to observe it once again,[16] and since the descendants of these representatives were also present in the days of Ezra, Am Yisroel *observed* the Yovel year after their return to Eretz Yisroel.[17]

Consequently, we see that in a time when there is no observance of Yovel as was the situation *before* Yirmiyohu brought back the representatives, then the statement מנו יובלות לקדש שמיטין applies.[18] On account of this there are Rishonim who pasken[32] that in a time such as nowadays when there is no observance of Yovel nevertheless

(13) Also not realizing that Yirmiyohu had brought back representatives see footnote (12).

(14) This is according to the way the Kesef Mishna[29b] learns and the Gemora understands that this is equally applicable to the days of Ezra.

(15) Meaning that every fiftieth year is counted as the fiftieth year of the old cycle, not the first year of the next cycle (see above no.3).

(16) According to Tosfos[31a] as a d'orysa, according to Rashi[31b] as a derabbonon, see Chapter One footnote (8).

(17) See footnote (16).

(18) Only after the representatives came back did they resume observing the Yovel year.

29b. שמיטה ויובל פ״י הל׳ ה׳. 30. הניחא לרבנן דאמרי שנת חמישים אינה מן המנין 31. הא ודאי דלא כרבי יהודה 31a. שם 31b. גיטין לו. ד״ה ״בשביעית בזמן הזה״ 32. ע״י רמב״ם שמיטה ויובל פ״י הל׳ ד׳

we have to count in the fiftieth year and only after this begin the count of the next Shmittoh Cycle. However the Geonim, who we pasken like,[33] learn that even the Rabbonon agree that when there is no *observance* of Yovel then midorysa there is no need to count a fiftieth year,[34][19] which should mean that before Yirmiyohu brought back representatives of each of the ten tribes, the tribes of Yehudah and Binyomin were *not* מנו יובלות לקדש שמיטין, This being so, then we have to understand why Rabbi Nachman Bar Yitzchok said that they were ?מנו יובלות לקדש שמיטין It is suggested[35] that this was due to the fact that during the exile of the ten tribes the remaining tribes of Yehudah and Binyomin were hoping that the ten tribes would return shortly as some in fact did when Yirmiyohu brought them back in the year 3303. They therefore did not alter the method of counting the years.[20] Another possibility[36] is that the exile was so short that a Yovel year never occurred during this period[21] that there should have been an alteration in the count.[37][22]

(19) The Geonim learn that when the Gemora concludes like the first assumption, that the statement מנו יובלות לקדש שמיטין by Rabbi Nachman Bar Yitzchok was according to the Rabbonon, it was merely concluding according to this assumption but the truth of the matter is that it cannot be even according to the Rabbonon (Kesef Mishna[34a]). The Kesef Mishna suggests that for the Geonim to have understood the Rabbonon as they do (which appears to oppose the simple meaning of the Gemora) they might have found some support for their view in a Gemora elsewhere.

(20) We see from this answer of the Kesef Mishna that even according to the Geonim that the din midorysa to count in the fiftieth year is only if there is an obligation to observe it, nevertheless in a period where it is not observed but it is *not* standing to have a lengthy nullification then they agree that there is still a din midorysa to count it. Only when there is going to be a more permanent period of non-observation of the Yovel years do they say that midorysa it is not to be counted.

(21) This, however, is seemingly difficult being that the exile was ninety-eight years (See "Shmittoh in General" Chapter Two no. 1).

(22) Although the Gemora states that when they were exiled the Yovel year became *nullified,* this means[37a] that since they were now exiled it was a period when the Yovel *should* become nullified *if* it would ever occur within this period.

After the Destruction, the prophet Yirmiyohu foretold that the Babylonian exile was to last for seventy years,[38] in which case the Yovel year would certainly occur within this period and since it would certainly become nullified they ceased to count with the inclusion of the Yovel year.

7. Counting the Shmittoh Cycle during the period of the Second Bais haMikdosh

It was mentioned above that even though there was now a *Kedusha Shniya* established in the Land, nevertheless it is questionable if the Shmittoh year was observed as an obligation midorysa or midrabbonon, depending on the individual views of Rebbi and the Rabbonon.[23] However it was also mentioned[24] that there is a difference of opinion amongst the Rishonim as to whether or not a nominal representation of each tribe living in Eretz Yisroel is sufficient to create an obligation midorysa to observe the Yovel year. According to the view that it is sufficient,[39] then it means that according to both Rebbi and the Rabbonon the Shmittoh year was observed as an obligation midorysa because when Ezra haSofer returned from the exile in Bovel he came back with descendants of those representatives of each tribe who were originally brought back by Yirmiyohu. Once again there was the condition of "כל יושביה", "all its inhabitants",[25] which renewed the obligation midorysa to observe the Yovel year. Thus even according to Rebbi there was an obligation midorysa to observe the Shmittoh year. Accordingly, this continued up until the destruction of the Second Bais haMikdosh, after which there were no longer representatives of all the tribes living in Eretz Yisroel and therefore the status of Shmittoh, it being midorysa or midrabbonon, would once again

(23) See Chapter One.[5*]
(24) See Chapter One footnote (8).
(25) See ibid.

38. ירמיה כה:יב 39. רבינו תם גיטין לו. ד"ה "בזמן"

become dependent on the individual views of Rebbi and the Rabbonon.

According to the view that these representatives were not sufficient to give an obligation midorysa to observe the Yovel year,[40] it was nevertheless enough to give an obligation miderabbonon, and is thus dependent on the individual views of Rebbi and the Rabbonon as to whether the obligation of Shmittoh was midorysa or miderabbonon.

Therefore during the period of the Second Bais haMikdosh they were obligated[(26)] to observe the Yovel year. We saw (above, no. 6) that during the years of the exile of the ten tribes they counted the Yovel years merely in order to keep a correct reckoning so as to sanctify the Shmittoh year in its appropriate time (מנו יובלות לקדש שמיטין). However even according to the view of the Geonim that after the First Destruction they continued to count the Shmittoh Cycle nevertheless they did not count the Yovel years[41(27)] which therefore means that when the period of the Second Bais haMikdosh began, they had to begin a new count of the Shmittoh Cycle, being that the previous count until now was missing the count of Yovel years, and so would not give a correct calculation of the fifty year Yovel cycle which they were now obligated to observe.[42]

(26) midorysa or miderabbonon.
(27) See above no. 6.

40. רש״י, עיין תוס׳ גיטין שם 41. עיין רמב״ם שמיטה ויובל פ״י הל׳ ה׳ 42. עיין חזו״א שביעית סימן ג׳ ס״ק ו׳

CHAPTER THREE
MELOCHOS

1. Avos and Toldos

Toldos of the primary (Avos) melochos have the same halocha of being forbidden on Shabbos. Had the Torah specified the prohibition of the thirty-nine Avos Melochos by stating each one clearly in the posuk rather than deriving them from the *hekesh* of the Mishkon (see "Shmittoh in General" no. 1), we would have then applied the rule of בנין אב[1] to derive directly from the posuk the equal prohibition of all the Toldos. However, being that the Avos here are linked with the Mishkon the assumption would be that the Torah is limiting its prohibition only to the acts as they were done in constructing the Mishkon.[2] In order to rule out such an assumption the Torah had to reveal to us elsewhere[1] that after having derived the prohibition of the thirty-nine melochos from the Mishkon they are in fact to act as a בנין אב so that all the derivatives are equally prohibited.

Consequently, it should mean that all the melochos, whether Avos or Toldos, should be classified under one heading, "The Forbidden Melochos". We find, however, that Chazal refer to them in the category of Av and Toldah. This is to point out[2] which melochos were those done in constructing the Mishkon,[3] Avos, and which melochos were not done in constructing the Mishkon,[4] Toldos.

(1)   When the Torah lays down a principle (Av) then it is merely serving as a prototype from which we are to build (בנין) everything which it means to forbid[1a] e.g. in forbidding זורע which is the concept of plant growth we would therefore derive that זומר (pruning which causes plant growth) is forbidden.

(2)   There being no mention of the act of זומר in constructing the Mishkon it would not be forbidden.

(3)   They were also a מלאכה חשובה, a melocha generally not omitted in the processing of a particular item.[2a]

(4)   Or are not a מלאכה חשובה.[2b]

1a. קצור כללים מי״ג מדות שהתורה נדרשת בהם מדה שלישית 1. ויקרא ד: ב ועיין שבת ע: וקג: 2. לפי שיטת רבי אליעזר בבא קמא ב. 2a. על פי חידושי הר״ן שבת עד. ד״ה "אמר אביי" 2b. לפי תירץ שני תוס׳ בבא קמא ב. ד״ה ה״ג

The Dispute Between Rashi and the Rambam

זומר (pruning) is forbidden on Shabbos but having not been done in constructing the Mishkon it therefore follows that it would be classified as a Toldah. This is in fact how Rashi[3] categorizes the melocha of זומר. The Rambam,[4] however, classifies זומר as an Av Melocha. Why is this so?

Both Rashi and the Rambam agree that the presence of the idea behind an action done in constructing the Mishkon is a required condition in order to be considered *doing* a melocha.[5]

What makes a melocha considered an Av according to Rashi is if the *action* which is accomplishing the idea is exactly the same action as was done in constructing the Mishkon to accomplish this idea. For instance, in accomplishing the idea of *plant growth* in constructing the Mishkon it was done by the act of placing seeds in soil.[5] זומר, however, was not an act found in constructing the Mishkon, therefore זומר according to Rashi is not an Av melocha but a Toldah.[6] The Rambam, agrees with Rashi that the presence of the idea behind an action is required so that the act is considered a melocha, nevertheless he understands that what classifies this action as being an Av melocha is if the same *idea behind it* was to be found behind an act in constructing the Mishkon. (Unlike Rashi where the act itself must be found in the Mishkon in order for it to be an Av.) From where did the Rambam draw support for this conclusion? From the concept of *Meleches Machsheves*. [6]

(5) In forbidding זורע the Torah is bringing it as a בניןאב (see footnote(1)) thus it is not merely telling us that sowing is prohibited it is telling us that an *act which causes plant growth* is forbidden.

(6) What makes it at least a Toldah is that it does have the same idea behind it as זורע.

3. שבת עג: ד"ה "כולן מלאכה אחת הן" 4. שבת פ"ז הל' ג' 5. מועד קטן ב: "דרכו של זורע לצמוחי פירא" 6. עיין מהרש"א סנהדרין כו. וע"ע באגלי טל מלאכת זורע סימן א' ס"ק ב' אות ו'

Meleches Machsheves I

We find concerning the construction of the Mishkon that the Torah[7] speaks of *Meleches Machsheves* (purposeful melocha) and by way of *hekesh* (see "Shmittoh in General" no. 1) this concept becomes involved with the melochos of Shabbos.[7a] By this the Torah tells us that in order for an act to be considered a melocha midorysa on Shabbos then one must not only perform an act which was done in constructing the Mishkon but he must do it with intention[7] (מחשבה). The Rambam understands that since it is *Meleches Machsheves* which the Torah forbids on Shabbos[8] then not only must one have מחשבה (doing the melocha consciously, not unwittingly) but also that it is the מחשבה *inherent in the act* (the general idea behind the melocha, such as sowing to cause plant growth, quite apart from the conscious intention for this outcome) which is what is primary in the melocha and thus categorizes the act as an Av. Therefore, according to the Rambam as long as an action leads to the idea which was found behind a melocha in constructing the Mishkon then it is an Av melocha even though it is not the same action as was done in constructing the Mishkon. Thus, even though the act of זומר which causes plant growth,[9] was not done in constructing the Mishkon, nevertheless causing plant growth was one of the ideas behind an action (זורע, sowing) done in constructing the Mishkon therefore the Rambam understands that זומר is an Av Melocha.

(7) Although the act must also have the same idea behind it as that in constructing the Mishkon, nevertheless, as is eminent from the discussion on מלאכה שצריכה לגופה (see no. 5) one need not have intention (מחשבה) for this. It is merely a condition that must be present to considered the act forbidden midorysa.

7. שמות לה: לג 7a. עיין רש״י ביצה יג: ד״ה "אלא מאי אית לך למימר" 8. מלאכת מחשבת אסרה תורה עי׳ ביצה יג: 9. רש״י שבת עג: ד״ה "כולן מלאכה אחת הן" ובמועד קטן ג. ד״ה "זמירה כלל זריעה"

Consequently we find that there are three levels concerning those melochos which are *not* listed among the thirty-nine Avos Melochos:[10]

1)If the melocha is the same type of act done with the same idea behind it as the melocha was done in constructing the Mishkon, then on account of both the former and the latter Rashi will classify it as an Av Melocha, and on account of the latter alone the Rambam will classify it as an Av Melocha.

Example: An Av Melocha done in constructing the Mishkon was זורע (sowing seeds). The idea behind זורע is to cause plant growth by the act of putting loose seeds into the soil. The melocha of מרכיב (grafting trees) was *not* a melocha done in constructing the Mishkon. However the act of מרכיב is putting something detached into something attached to cause growth, therefore being exactly the same action and idea as זורע. Then even though the action to cause growth here is done with branches instead of seeds nevertheless Rashi[11] still classifies it is an Av Melocha. According to the Rambam[12] it is an Av Melocha merely from the fact that it has the same idea behind it as זורע.

2)If the melocha has the same idea behind it but is done with a slight deviation from the "action" of a melocha done in constructing the Mishkon yet the deviation is to such a small extent that it is not enough to make it considered a completely different action from the action of the melocha in the Mishkon, then Rashi still classifies it as an Av Melocha, and again the Rambam classifies it as an Av Melocha because it has the same idea behind it.

Example: An Av Melocha done in constructing the Mishkon was חורש (ploughing). The idea behind חורש is to soften the ground[13] to make it suitable for sowing.[14] The melocha of חופר (digging holes in soil) was not a melocha done in constructing the Mishkon (because

---

10. על פי כללת שבת כללי ל״ט מלאכות אות א׳ .11 שם .12 שבת פ״ז הל׳ ג׳ וט׳ .13 מועד קטן ב: "מה דרכו של חורש לרפויי ארעא" .14 מאירי שבת עג. "לרפות הארץ להיותה ראויה לזריעה"

digging holes is not exactly the same act as ploughing). However, digging a hole in the soil with the idea of softening it to place a seed in it is similar to חורש in that it has the same idea behind it, but done with a slight deviation in practice from חורש, but not enough to consider it an entirely different action. Therefore Rashi[15] still classifies חופר as an Av Melocha. The Rambam[16] classifies it as an Av Melocha merely because it has the same idea behind it as חורש, without considering the degree of similarity between חופר and חורש.

3)If the melocha has the same idea behind it as a Melocha done in constructing the Mishkon, but in practice deviates to the extent that it is considered as being an entirely different act then Rashi will classify it as a Toldah, but the Rambam will still classify it as an Av Melocha, and the example of this is the melocha of זומר, discussed above, since זומר is radically different in practice from זורע.

What is classified as a Toldah according to the Rambam?

The Rambam learns[17] that if the Melocha is not done with the body of the plant then it is a Toldah.

Example: המשקה צמחים (watering plants) was not a melocha done in constructing the Mishkon. Even though it is an entirely different action from זורע, nevertheless since at least it has the same idea behind it as זורע in that it causes plant growth, therefore Rashi[18] classifies it as a Toldah. The Rambam[19] here agrees that it is not an Av Melocha because the cause of growth is done by means of water and not by means of handling the body of the plant.

In respect to Hilchos Shmittoh, the Torah does not involve the concept of *Meleches Machsheves*.[20] Therefore even the Rambam would agree that an Av Melocha in Shmittoh would only refer to the actual act referred to in the Torah. Actions which are done with the same idea behind the principle, but not the form, merely defines

15. שבת מו: ד"ה "איסורא דאורייתא" על פי אגלי טל מלאכת חורש סימן א' ס"ק ב' ד"ה "ואחד"
16. שבת פ"ז הל' ב'. 17. על פי כללת שבת שם 18. מועד קטן ג. ד"ה "תולדות" 19. שבת פ"ח הל' ב'. תוס' מועד קטן ג. סוף ד"ה "נטיבה" ובגיטין מד: ד"ה "שנתקוצה" ובסנהדרין כו. ד"ה "לעקל"

what are considered Toldos of this Av. Thus we find that the Rambam[21] quotes the text of the Gemora[22] which implies that זומר during Shmittoh should be classified as a Toldah. It is only on account of the fact that it is written clearly in the posuk that it is considered an Av.[8]

2. Status of the Melochos of Shmittoh

Based on an analysis of the p'sukim where the four melochos (זורע, זומר, קוצר, בוצר) prohibited during Shmittoh are mentioned, other melochos forbidden by the Torah during Shmittoh are derived. Exactly which melochos are included is however disputed amongst both the Tannoim and Amoroim.

The various possible ways to analyze the p'sukim are more easily understood if they are divided in the following way.

A. ושבתה הארץ שבת לד׳

B. שש שנים תזרע שדך

C. ובשנה השביעית שבת שבתון יהיה לארץ

D. שדך לא תזרע וכרמך לא תזמר לא תקצור לא תבצר

E. שנת שבתון יהיה לארץ

These p'sukim are divided into five parts. For the benefit of having a quick reference throughout the coming discussions the following chart may be used:

---

(8) The Gemora[22a] states that זומר in Hilchos Shmittoh is an Av because it is written in the posuk (seeריטב״א[22b] and below no. 2). The Rambam here quotes the text of the Gemora and no more and therefore could well understand it as does the ריטב״א (being that the ריטב״א in his understanding eliminates problems in the text) in that זומר *would have been a Toldah* in Hilchos Shmittoh had it not been stated in the posuk. One can understand the אגלי טל[22c] as learning this same way.

---

21. שמיטה ויובל פ״א הל׳ ג׳ ועיין ברדב״ז שם 22. מועד קטן ג. 22a. שם b22. ריטב״א מועד קטן שם 22c. זורע סימן א׳ ס״ק ב׳ אות ו׳

		(A) לאכול האכילה כסדר	(B) זמן חיוב הביעור של	(C) זמן חיוב ביעור הפירות לאחר	(D) זמן חיוב ביעור אם לא אכלו ולא ביערו בזמן	(E) זמן הביעור לאכול
דברי	אבב				מקום וחיוב לאכל	
	ירקגינה			לאכל	פטו	לאכל
	זרעין				מקום וחיוב לאכל	
ירקשדה	ר אילנות	חורב הכלל זמן			אצא זמן לכלל	
	ר יהנו א ידוע				מקום וחיוב לאכל	
	ר יהנו אם הגיע	תעשה	תעשה			
	ר יהנו	תעשה	תעשה			
	ר סבו	חורב הכלל תעשה			הבסל הבסל	

The Bavli

Rova (an Amora) states[23] that during the Shmittoh year the Torah forbids the Avos Melochos but not the Toldos (this will be explained). This is derived from the fact that the Torah (in section D) mentions four melochos which are forbidden, זורע, זומר, קוצר, בוצר. Now, had the Torah just mentioned the two melochos of זורע וקוצר then I would assume that they are a בנין אב to derive from them similar melochos. Accordingly, the concept of זורע being to cause plant growth would tell me that the melocha of זומר is also forbidden midorysa. In the same vein since the concept of קוצר (reaping) is to detach a plant from its natural source of growth then this would tell me that the melocha of בוצר (picking grapes) is forbidden midroysa. The Torah, however, specifically mentions זומר ובוצר despite their derivitability from זורע וקוצר. Therefore Rova deduces by way of this redundancy that the Torah is not setting down these melochos as examples, but are meant very literally, only זורע, זומר, קוצר, ובוצר. are forbidden by the Torah during Shmittoh.[9] By the fact that the Torah states זומר ובוצר then they are in this instance principles[10] (Avos) *and* we have learned from the aforementioned redundancy that it is only these four melochos which are forbidden during Shmittoh, therefore it becomes clear that only Avos Melochos are forbidden.

We now understand why during Shmittoh it is only זומר ובוצר of all the Toldos of Hilchos Shabbos, which are forbidden Midorysa during Shmittoh.[24] All the other melochos which are Toldos in Hilchos Shabbos remain Toldos in Hilchos Shmittoh and are therefore permitted midorysa.[25]

---

(9) By the Torah mentioning just זומר and בוצר it is ממעט (excludes) all the other melochos which are Toldos in Hilchos Shabbos.

(10) Anything stated in the Torah is a principle, see footnote (1)

23. מועד קטן שם 24. לפי הריטב״א מועד קטן שם 25. ריטב״א שם

The Bnei haYeshiva now ask Rova: Surely we have a Beraisa[11] from where we see that all the other melochos are also forbidden midorysa? The Beraisa brings the following drosha to derive this fact:[26][12]

In section D, rather than placing the word "לא" ("you shall not") *before* the word "שדך" "your field" and before the word "כרמך" "your vineyard" that it should read "you shall not (sow) your field and you shall not (prune) your vineyard", the Torah places the word "לא" *after* the words "שדך" and "כרמך", reading "your field *you shall not...*" "your vineyard *you shall not...*" inferring that *all* melocha in your field and vineyard is forbidden i.e. "your field you shall not (do *any* work to as *well* as to) sow". "Your vineyard you shall not (do *any* work to as *well* as to) prune". Thus there is a clear indication from the drosha that all agricultural melochos are forbidden midorysa. This would be problematic for (the Amora) Rova.[13] Rova answers that apart from the four melochos of זורע, זומר, קוצר בוצר all the melochos are forbidden miderabbonon and the Beraisa is bringing the drosha which the Rabbonon merely use as their *Asmachta*. Thus we have one Amora, Rova, who learns that only four melochos are forbidden by a negative commandment[14] during the Shmittoh year, all other agricultural melochos being forbidden miderabbonon.

(11)   A Tannaic statement which was not included in the compilation of the Mishnayos by Rabbeinu haKodosh.25a
(12)   Being that there is the implication of the aforementioned redundancy brought by Rova which as explained prevents deriving that all melochos are forbidden by way of בנין אב, the only way to now derive that all other melochos are forbidden is to find another way of learning the posuk which shows that there is no such redundancy in the posuk.
(13)   If it would not be for this drosha of "לא" then Rova's redundancy would have to be agreed to.
(14)   Unlike a positive commandment, for transgressing a negative commandment one receives the punishment of malkus.

Rabbi Elozor and Rabbi Yochanon

The Gemora goes on to bring a dispute between two Amoroim, Rabbi Elozor and Rabbi Yochanon, whether or not all the other agricultural melochos are forbidden by a negative commandment.[15] Rabbi Elozor[16] learns that they are forbidden by a negative commandment.[17] The Gemora suggests that his view is based on the following way of examining the parts of the posuk mentioned above.

The p'sukim are written in such a way that sections CDE make up a sequence to which the rule of כלל ופרט וכלל[18] can be applied.[27] That is, section C forbids *all* melocha in general (כלל) as it says "in the seventh year there shall be a rest (in general) to the land." The Torah, however, goes on to bring section D which now specifies (פרט) that the melochos which are forbidden during Shmittoh are sowing, pruning, reaping grain and picking grapes as it says "your field you shall not *sow* and your vineyard you shall not *prune* ...you shall not *harvest* etc". Yet the Torah then concludes with section E which again clearly expresses a prohibition of melocha in general (כלל) as it says "it shall be a year of rest (in general) to the land".

---

(15) Although the Gemora only states the question with regard to the melocha of חורש (ploughing) nevertheless it is only stated as an example as is clear from the further discussion of the Gemora. The Chazon Ish[26a] learns that this was used as an example because of the chidush which it involves i.e. even though the particular melocha of חורש does have a special positive commandment forbidding it whether from the posuk "בחריש ובקציר" or from הלכה למשה מסיני (see below; in learning from here that it is forbidden even before Shmittoh it tells us that it is certainly forbidden during Shmittoh[26b]) nevertheless there is still an opinion that there is no negative commandment forbidding it.

(16) This is according to the Yerushalmi [26c] that it is Rabbi Yochanan who learns that they are not forbidden by a negative commandment. However according to Tosfos[26d] it is questionable which way each Amora learns.

(17) Thus he must learn the posuk in a way that it cancels out Rova's understanding of the posuk. See footnote (12).

(18) First a general term, then a specific term, then again a general term.

26a. שביעית י"ז ס"ק א' 26b. חזו"א שם ד"ה "מיהו" 26c. כלאים פ"ח הל' א' 26d. מועד קטן ג:
ד"ה "רבי" 27. לפי פירש"י שם ד"ה "כל מקום וגו'"

The rule of such a pattern is that we may derive a prohibition of any melocha which resembles the specifications (פרט). Therefore just as the Torah here in its פרט forbids four melochos which involve working the land and trees, so also it reveals to us that all (כלל) other melochos which involve working the land and trees are also forbidden.[28(19)]

Rabbi Yochanon does not make this derivation because he understands that section D is not the usual type of specification (פרט) where it can make up the pattern of כלל ופרט וכלל because in section D the specifications are such that they give rise to the questions mentioned before in the statement of Rova. That is, why does the Torah here need to specify זומר ובוצר if it anyway mentions זורע וקוצר (see above)? Therefore rather than coming as a פרט they are coming as a מיעוט (minimization) that it is only these four melochos which are forbidden during Shmittoh and no other melochos. Consequently Rabbi Yochanon does not learn that there is a כלל ופרט וכלל at all here, thus all other agricultural melochos are not included in this negative command and thereby do not carry the penalty of malkus.

The Yerushalmi [29]

The Talmud Yerushalmi's understanding of the dispute between Rabbi Yochanon and Rabbi Elozor is slightly different from that of the Bavli.

---

(19) From the fact that Rabbi Elozor here learns that the other melochos are forbidden midorysa, then it means that his view is that the drosha from "לא" brought in the Beraisa earlier is in fact not an *Asmachta* for a din miderabbonon but is a drosha for the din midorysa, if so why does he not bring the drosha of "לא"? The ריטב"א answers that the Beraisa was not precise, the real drosha being the כלל ופרט וכלל

Rather than picking out sections CDE to have the pattern of כלל ופרט וכלל like the Bavli wants to suggest, the Yerushalmi proposes that Rabbi Elozor derives that the other agricultural melochos[20] are forbidden by a negative command during Shmittoh by way of another pattern[21] which is found in this parsha.

That is, it is written in such a way that sections A and D make up a sequence to which the rule of "דבר שהיה בכלל ויצא מן הכלל"[22] can be applied i.e.:

Section A forbids *all* melocha in general, as it says: "then the land shall rest in honour of Hashem". Therefore this includes the four melochos זורע, זומר, קוצר, בוצר thus they are the דבר (the subject) which are in the כלל. However comes section D which now mentions these four melochos separately (ויצא מן הכלל), as it says "your field you shall not *sow* etc."

The rule for such a pattern is like the rule of כלל ופרט וכלל, that the Torah comes to reveal that there is a prohibition of any melocha which is similar to the specifications mentioned.[23] Therefore just as זורע, זומר, קוצר, בוצר are melochos which involve working the land and trees and are prohibited here by a negative command, so also *all* other melochos which involve working the land and trees are forbidden, and carry the penalty of malkus.

Rabbi Yochonon

The Yerushalmi mentions two reasons why Rabbi Yochonon does not make this derivation. The first proposal is that he is of the opinion that since the prohibition of section A is phrased as a

---

(20) See footnote (15).

(21) Thereby cancelling the implication of the seeming redundancy of זומר ובוצר.

(22) When a subject which is already included in a general term is afterwards mentioned in order to give some new information, it is not meant to be an isolated instance but to clarify the general term as well.

(23) The reason why sections A and D are not considered as making a pattern of כלל ופרט (a general term followed by a specific term, in which case the general rule is qualified and limited to the specifications and *no more*) is because[29a] section D is not written *immediately* after section A.

29a. נדה לג.תעיין בקיצור כללים מי"ג מדות שהתורה נדרשת בהם מדה שמינית

'positive' commandment while the prohibition of section D takes the form of a 'negative' commandment, they are therefore different types of prohibitions and cannot be learned one from the other i.e. we cannot apply the rule of "דבר שהיה בכלל ויצא מן הכלל", therefore we are left with Rova's redundancy and the other melochos cannot be included in the prohibition. Rabbi Elozor, however, is of the view that though they are different types of prohibitions, nevertheless they both deal with the same subject, the prohibition of melocha during the Shmittoh year, and the application of דבר שהיה בכלל ויצא מן הכלל is still possible. The other melochos can therefore be included in those melochos prohibited during Shmittoh.

Rabbi Bo from Krosignayar, in dispute of the aforementioned, has another way of understanding Rabbi Yochonon. Granted that even though they are two different types of prohibitions nevertheless they can be learned one from the other. There is however another posuk telling us that there is no penalty of malkus for the other melochos.

Section B says "six years sow your field, and six years prune your vineyard" implying that during the seventh year it is forbidden. In a case like this where a negative commandment is implied from a positive commandment, the negative commandment is categorized as being like a positive commandment, in that it does not carry the penalty of malkus. Thus, at this stage, the Torah gives a positive commandment not to sow or prune during Shmittoh. Such a positive commandment, however, is already evident from section A as it says "then the land shall rest", melocha *in general* being forbidden. Why, then, is the positive commandment duplicated by section B? Had the Torah omitted section B, then we would learn section A as making up the pattern of דבר שהיה בכלל ויצא מן הכלל together with section D just like Rabbi Elozor wants to, and therefore as well as all other melochos being forbidden by this positive commandment they are also forbidden as a negative commandment. However on account of the doubling up of the positive commandment in section B it therefore emphasises a negation of the derivation of the negative commandment in section D, so that all the other melochos are only forbidden by their positive commandment and do *not* carry the penalty of malkus.[30]

Rabbi Elozor, on the other hand, does not learn from section B the implication that Rabbi Yochonon learns from it, there therefore being no duplication of a positive commandment the rule of דבר שהיה בכלל ויצא מן הכלל can be applied from which we learn that the other melochos are mentioned as negative commandments and carry the penalty of malkus.

The Dispute Between Rabbi Yirmiyah and Rabbi Yossi

The Yerushalmi also mentions a difference of opinion between two Tannoim regarding the other melochos.

Rabbi Yirmiyah's opinion is like the opinion of Rabbi Yochonon[31] that the other melochos are included in the positive commandment not to do melocha during Shmittoh. Therefore the other melochos do not carry the penalty of malkus.

Rabbi Yossi, on the other hand, learns that there is not even a positive commandment against other melochos, therefore, the prohibition of the other melochos during Shmittoh is only miderabbonon. The Gemora questions this opinion of Rabbi Yossi, surely there is section A "then the land shall rest" which is a positive commandment not to do any other melochos? Rabbi Yossi answers that since section A is followed later by section D which specifies the prohibition of זורע, זומר, קוצר, בוצר then it is only these four melochos which are included in this positive commandment. Rabbi Elozor,[(24)] on the other hand, learns that section D comes as a יצא מן הכלל to specify that all melocha is forbidden from a negative commandment.

---

(24) One of the two Amoroim discussed before.

Consequently, we now have two Tannoim, Rabbi Yirmiyah and Rabbi Yossi, who both learn that the other melochos do *not* carry the penalty of malkus. If so, how can Rabbi Elozor, an Amora, dispute this and learn that the other melochos do carry the penalty of malkus?

The Gemora goes on to bring part of a Beraisa where a Tanna states "It might have been presumed that there is the penalty of malkus for Tosfos"(25) (lit. "addition") This implies that the penalty of malkus for Tosfos is only a *presumption* and that the conclusion is that there is *no* penalty of malkus for "Tosfos". What is meant by "Tosfos"?

Rabbi Elozor learns that "Tosfos" in the Beraisa refers to "Tosfos Shviyis" the period of prohibition of melocha prior to and in 'addition' to the Shmittoh year.(26) Thus the Tanna is concluding that there is only no penalty of malkus for doing melocha during this period of Tosfos Shviyis, but during Shmittoh itself melocha such as חורש does carry the penalty of malkus.(27) Therefore Rabbi Elozor draws support for his view that there is a penalty of malkus for the other melochos from the Tanna of this Beraisa.

The Positive Commandment Concerning חורש(28)
Rabbi Akiva

Although Rabbi Elozor (an Amora) will learn that the view of Rabbi Akiva (a Tanna) is that there is a negative commandment midorysa forbidding the melocha of חורש[32] nevertheless there is a

---

(25) While discussing the Yerushalmi, the Yerushalmi's pronunciation "Tosfos", not "Tosefes" is being used.

(26) See Chapter Four.

(27) Rabbi Yochanon learns[31a] that when the Beraisa here says "Tosfos" it refers to the melocha of חורש (and to any of the other melochos which are Toldos in Hilchos Shabbos) and it is called "Tosfos" because being a melocha which is not stated clearly in the Torah as being forbidden therefore it is being *added* to what has clearly been stated. Thus the Tanna is saying that there is no malkus for חורש and other melochos.

(28) Unlike the discussion above, this only concerns the melocha of חורש and not the other melochos.

31a. פני משה 32. ירושלמי שם "פתר לה שביעית דרבי לעזר" עיין פני משה

seperate discussion in the Gemora showing that Rabbi Akiva derives that there is also a positive commandment forbidding the particular melocha of חורש.

The Gemora[33] discusses a difference of opinion concerning the subject of "תוספת שביעית" (Tosefes Shviyis, see chapter four) Rabbi Akiva learns that the posuk[34] which says "בחריש ובקציר תשבות" "(from involvement) in ploughing and reaping you shall rest" is a positive commandment and comes to tell us that there is a prohibition against ploughing beginning a certain period *before* the commencement of Shmittoh (see ibid for details). Now if there is a prohibition of חורש even before the Shmittoh year then it goes without saying that this would also tell us that it is prohibited during the Shmittoh year.[35] Therefore even if we were to conclude like Rabbi Yossi in the Yerushalmi mentioned above that the positive commandment of "ושבתה הארץ" only refers to the four melochos of זורע, זומר, קוצר, בוצר, nevertheless we now learn that according to Rabbi Akiva there is a positive commandment against ploughing during Shmittoh from "בחריש ובקציר". Rabbi Yishmoel[36] argues with Rabbi Akiva and learns that the posuk of בחריש ובקציר "תשבות" speaks only of Shabbos (see ibid for details). However Rabbi Yishmoel learns that there is nevertheless a prohibition against ploughing before the Shmittoh year, and this is a הלכה למשה מסיני (a halocha which was orally given over to Moshe Rabbeinu on Har Sinai from Hashem, with no known source in the Written Law). Again, it would follow from this that ploughing *during* Shmittoh should certainly be forbidden.

3. זורע indoors

The Gemora[37] poses the following question. On the one hand the posuk concerning Shmittoh says[38] "...ושבתה הארץ שבת לד'" "and the

33. מועד קטן ג:ד. 34. שמות לד: כא 35. כללכת שביעית עמוד מג וחזו"א שביעית סימן י"ז ס"ק א' ד"ה "מיהו" 36. מועד קטן שם 37. ירושלמי ערלה פ"א סוף הל' ב' 38. ויקרא כה: ב

land shall rest in honour of HaShem" implying that it is prohibited to do melocha on the land of Eretz Yisroel *wheresoever* it may be, even if it is the ground of a house with a roof over it and is not a field outside. However another posuk says[39] שדך לא תזרע וכרמך לא תזמור "your *field* you shall not sow, and your *vineyard* you shall not prune", implying that the issur melocha during the Shmittoh year is only in an open area such as a field and a vineyard but not if it is the ground inside a house. The Gemora remains with the question. This means that if the observance of Shmittoh nowadays is midorysa then we apply the rule of ספק דאורייתא לחומרא (when there is a doubt whether something is forbidden midorysa then we are stringent and forbid it) and it is forbidden to sow in the earthen floor of a house. However the Pe'as HaShulchon[40] writes that since Shmittoh today is miderabbonon[(29)] therefore we can be lenient and allow sowing in the earthen ground of a house. The Chazon Ish,[41] who also paskens that Shmittoh today is miderabbonon[42] writes that we can only allow sowing in a non-perforated flowerpot inside a house, but not in the floor itself (see below).

Roof Garden

The Rosh[43] is of the opinion that if earth is laying on top of the roof of a house then sowing in this earth is the same as sowing outdoors since it is connected to the ground by means of its connection to the house. Coupled with the fact that this is considered a normal method of sowing, it is therefore forbidden midorysa.

4. Flowerpots

If a flowerpot of earth is positioned on the ground outside and there is a perforation on the bottom of it[(30)] (large enough for an

---

(29) So that even sowing in a field is only an issur miderabbonon.
(30) or even if it is at the side of the pot providing it is paralleling some part of the planted root.[43a]

39. שם: ד 40. שם: סימן כ' (א') ס"ק נ"ב 41. שביעית סימן כ"ב ס"ק א' 42. שם סימן ג' ס"ק ח' 43.
שו"ת הרא"ש כלל ב' ס"ק ד' 43a. רש"י שבת צה. ד"ה "התולש מעציץ נקוב חייב", ואגלי טל קוצר
סימן ב' ומ"ב סימן של"ו ס"ק מ"ב ועיין בשעה"צ ס"ק ל"ו

olive to fall through[44]) then the earth inside the pot is considered as the ground itself and therefore it is forbidden to sow in the flowerpot.[31] If the flowerpot has no perforation on its side or bottom so that it is not directly connected to the ground (unlike the case of a roof garden), then it is not considered connected to the ground, because unlike a house a pot is moveable, and also it is not considered a usual way for people to sow,[45] that it should be called *sowing in the ground,* it should therefore be permissible midorysa to sow in the pot. The Rabbonon, however, made a gezera (decree) that one must not sow in such a pot in order to prevent one from mistakenly thinking that one can also sow outside in a perforated pot.[46][32] Consequently, if Shmittoh today is midorysa so that the ground inside a house is considered as having the same din as a field, then it would certainly be forbidden to sow in a perforated flowerpot standing on the earthen ground inside a house, and the gezera miderabbonon not to sow even in a non-perforated pot standing on the earthen ground inside a house may[33] also apply.

However as mentioned above, the Chazon Ish writes that since today Shmittoh is miderabbonon therefore concerning a non-perforated pot standing on the earthen ground inside a house it is permissible to sow in it (and do all other agricultural melochos in it)

(31) According to most Rishonim this is even if the flowerpot is by some means suspended in the air over the ground [44a] because it can still draw a little bit of nourishment from the ground below.[44b]

(32) The Chazon Ish[46a] discusses the possibility that since this *gezera* is only mentioned concerning the dinim of Ma'aseros therefore it may not necessarily apply to the dinim of Shviyis.

(33) See footnote (32).

44. עוקצין פ״ב מ״י ועיין מאירי שבת צה. וע״ע בחזו״א שם ד״ה ״ובין״ 44a. עיין אגלי טל זורע סימן ד׳ 44b. הגהות אשרי שבת פא: 45. שו״ת הרא״ש שם 46. גזרינן אינו נקוב אטו נקוב, על פי רדב״ז שמיטה ויובל פ״א הל׳ ו׳ עיין חזו״א שם ד״ה ״נראה״ 46a. שם

and this is certainly so when it is standing on ground covered by stone.[34] This applies even if the pot is made of a permeable material such as earthenware except in the case where one wants to plant a tree in it, because being that its roots are very powerful they can penetrate through it and draw nourishment from the earthen floor.[47] According to one opinion[48] this is even in the case of a wooden flowerpot (which is seemingly less permeable than earthenware).

If part of the plant in a non-perforated flowerpot projects out of the pot, extending above the ground below then there is a view that the entire plant in the pot is considered as growing in the ground.[49] So too if the pot is filled right up until its very top there is a view that it is then like a perforated pot.[50]

II מלאכת מחשבת and (intention) כוונה .5

In areas other than Hilchos Shabbos there is a dispute amongst the Tannoim with regard to the role of intention when transgressing a Torah prohibition.[51] Unintentional acts in areas which the Torah prohibits (דבר שאינו מתכוין) are considered, according to Rabbi Yehudah, as a full violation, while according to Rabbi Shimon they are not considered a violation at all. The halocha is like Rabbi Shimon.[52] This is in general. With regard to Shabbos, however, Rabbi Yehudah agrees that it is not forbidden midorysa. It is still prohibited, however, miderabbonon.[53] Rabbi Shimon will, as in other areas, maintain that there has been no violation whatsoever.[54]

---

(34) However some say that it is possible that due to the fact that the covering of the floor is fixed directly over the earth beneath it then any sowing in earth which is on top of this covering (such as earth in עציץ נקוב) is considered as actually sowing in the earth under the covering.[46b]

46b. כרם ציון הלכות פסוקות פ״ב הערה ב׳ 47. ירושלמי ערלה שם ועיין רמב״ם מעשר שני פ״י הל׳ ח׳ 48. גר״א יו״ד סימן רצ״ד אות ס״ד 49. עיין אגלי טל מלאכת קוצר סימן ג׳ 50. חיי אדם הל׳ שבת כלל י״ב ס״ק ב׳ 51. עי׳ כלאים פ״ט מ״ה, שבת כט: ותוס׳ שם מא: ד״ה ״מיחם״ 52.רמב״ם כלאים פ״י הל׳ ט״ז, מחבר יו״ד סימן ש״א סעיף ו׳ 53. פטור אבל אסור ועיין בתוס׳ יומא לד:ד״ה ״רבי״ ובשבת מא: ד״ה ״מיחם״ 54. פטור ומותר

Meleches Machsheves, that work must be intentional and purposeful, is why Rabbi Yehudah distinguishes between Hilchos Shabbos and other areas.[35] The Rambam[55] decides according to the opinion of Rabbi Shimon, that work done on Shabbos without intent carries no guilt with it even miderabbonon.

For example: Making a furrow in a field is חורש (ploughing). It is permissable however, to pull a bench over a field even though a furrow may form, so long as it is not a certainty[36] (i.e., the bench is not overly heavy) and he has no intention to form the furrow.

Before arriving at a full definition as to what is considered "intention", it is first necessary to discuss and define the concept of מלאכה שצריכה לגופה.

מלאכה שצריכה לגופה

There is another dispute between Rabbi Shimon and Rabbi Yehudah.[56] There are two factors, *Mishkon* (work as done in construction of it) and *machshova* (intent, derived from *Meleches Machsheves*) which are an integral part of a melocha midorysa (see see above no. 1). Rabbi Shimon reasons[57] that in coupling these two factors together[37] we may derive another condition required in order to be considered a melocha midorysa. That is, in performing an act one must *intend* (*machshova*) to do it for the *purpose* (גוף) for which it was *needed* (צריכה) in the Mishkon. This is מלאכה שצריכה לגופה. For instance, the melocha of זורע in constructing the Mishkon was an *act* of placing seeds in the soil (which is a cause of plant growth[38]) for the *purpose* of having plants, (these were then

(35) According to Rabbi Shimon *Meleches Machsheves* creates a requirement for מלאכה שצריכה לגופה (see below).
(36) It is not פסיק רישא see below.
(37) This is according to Tosfos[57a] who understands that מלאכה שצריכה לגופה is linked with *Mishkon*, unlike Rashi.[57b]
(38) This being the idea behind sowing.

55. שבת פ״א הל׳ ה׳. 56. שבת צג. ותוס׳ שם צד. ד״ה ״רבי״. 57. לפי תוס׳ שם שלא כמו רש״י שם צג: ד״ה ״רבי שמעון פטור״ 57a. שם 57b. שם

used as dyes an *end* purpose, but *not* the purpose discussed here) for colouring the curtains of the Mishkon. Thus in a case where one would intentionally place seeds in the soil (an act which causes plant growth) but without intending to do it for the purpose of having plants e.g. he merely wants to fill up a hole in the ground by using seeds, then this is מלאכה שאינה צריכה לגופה [39] (a melocha done without intent for the purpose needed in the Mishkon) not a melocha midorysa according to Rabbi Shimon.[40] Rabbi Yehudah, disagrees with Rabbi Shimon, with the view that we can only go so far as deriving *intended action* from the factors Mishkon and *machshova* but not מלאכה שצריכה לגופה therefore in the case just mentioned being that one intended to perform the act of sowing which causes plant growth, it is enough already to classify it as a melocha midorysa.[41] The Rambam[58] concludes like Rabbi Yehudah. Most Poskim, nevertheless, pasken like Rabbi Shimon,[59] that it is not a melocha midorysa, however it is forbidden miderabbonon.[60]

פסיק רישא

"Intention" however must be further defined before arriving at a full definition of *Meleches Machsheves*. It was mentioned above that pulling a bench along a field on Shabbos in a way that it does not

---

(39) Providing that he does this in someone else's field in which case it is לא ניחה ליה. (ניחה ליה) is benefiting from the purpose of the melocha, in this case having a plant. Filling a hole is therefore not ניחה ליה, if however done in his own field it is ניחה ליה since he will eventually benefit from having a plant).

(40) If after having done the melocha, one has a change of mind and decides to use the plants which grow from the seeds, he has not transgressed because *Meleches Machsheves* says that what happens later is not enough, intention at the time the melocha is performed being necessary.

(41) Causing plant growth, which is the idea behind sowing is a condition required to be present merely for the *action* of sowing to be forbidden midorysa, therefore having no intention for this idea does not prevent the action from being considered a melocha midorysa.

---

58. שבת פ"י הל' י"ט. ועיין במחבר סימן שט"ז סעיף ח' 59. עיין מ"ב סימן שט"ז ס"ק ל"ד 60. מ"ב שם (היינו פטור אבל אסור)

necessarily make a furrow is permitted because it is a דבר שאינו מתכוין i.e. a furrow was made but one had no intention to make it. However, if a person pulled a very heavy bench along the field so that even though he personally has no intention of making a furrow nevertheless the outcome is unavoidable i.e. he will definitely do the melocha (termed "פסיק רישא"[42]), Tosfos[61] then learns that in such a case even Rabbi Shimon (who normally is lenient with regard to דבר שאינו מתכוין, see above) will agree that this is considered as having had the intention to make a furrow because the person in such a situation knows only too well that a furrow will be dug. Therefore it is considerd that he has done the 'action' of חורש with intention (i.e. פסיק רישא has made it a דבר המתכוין). However, it would still be a מלאכה שאינו צריכה לגופה and exempt, since the person has no need for the furrow, he merely wants to move his bench to a new location.

ניחא ליה, לא ניחא ליה

Whether his act would indeed be termed צריכה לגופה would depend on whether he benefitted from the furrow (ניחא לי) or not, (לא ניחא לי). Should he be dragging the bench on his *own* field, thereby benefitting from it in that the ground is being softened in advance of planting then it would be evident[62] that this also has intention and the moving of the bench to a new location is also an

---

(42) "פסיק רישא" is an abbreviated form of the phrase "פסיק רישא ולא ימות" (שבת עה) "cut off its head but let it not die". This is used to express that just as it is impossible to cut off the head of a living being without it dying, so also if it is impossible to perform an act without it also being considered a melocha then it is forbidden.

61. שבת עה. ד"ה "טפי" וקג. ד"ה "לא" 62. אנן סהדי

act of intentional ploughing. i.e. מלאכה שצריכה לגופה(43)

 We now know that *Meleches Machsheves* governs the factor of intention in three areas:

1) awareness that the act is being done (כוונה)

2) that the outcome of the act is needed (מלאכה שצריכה לגופה).

3) that an unavoidable outcome (פסיק רישא) is considered as having been intended, even if that is not the purpose of the melocha.

---

(43) It is forbidden miderabbonon because the melocha here is not being done כדרכה (in the usual manner, פסיק רישא is forbidden even in a matter concerning a derabbonon62a). Where he pulls the bench along someone else's field then it would remain at being a מלאכה שאינה צריכה לגופה and exempt even if it had been כדרכה, however it is forbidden miderabbonon. According to Rabbi Yehudah sinceמלאכה שאינה צריכה לגופה is no factor then it is forbidden midorysa because being a פסיק רישא it is an act of ploughing with intent.

CHART OF AGRICULTURAL MELOCHOS

The following is a list of the melochos which are forbidden during the Shmittoh year. The intention of this list is also to give the reader who is learning Mishnayos Shviyis an opportunity to have somewhat of a chart to refer to, which will aid him in his learning. Therefore the Perek and the Mishna where each melocha is discussed in the mishnayos is quoted in parenthesis. What has been classified as Avos and Toldos is in line with the view of Rashi (see above, no. 1). For simplicity this list is based upon what are Avos and Toldos in Hilchos Shabbos. Where in Hilchos Shmittoh there is a variant it will be mentioned in a footnote.

חורש: (פ״א מ״א) Ploughing:

Purpose: The idea behind the Av Melocha of חורש is for:

1) ריפוי ארעא[1]   Softening the earth.[2] This is done in order to make it suitable for having seeds sown within it.[3]

2) יפוי ארעא[4]   Improvement[(1)] of the earth.[5] This is also done in order to make it suitable for having seeds sown within it.[6(2)]

---

(1) ״יפוי״ here does not mean beautification but—"benefit-improvement".[4a]

(2) When the Rambam[6a] lists melochos such as מקרסם (see below "c") which are for יפוי ארעא and calls them a *Toldah* of חורש this is because though יפוי ארעא is the idea behind the principle (Av) of ploughing nevertheless these cannot be Avos because they are not done with the body of the earth (see above no: 1). When the Rambam goes on to speak of המשוה פני השדה (see below "h") then being done with the body of the earth this is considered an Av.[6b] Rashi would still consider this as a Toldah being that it is not the same action as חורש, the אגלי טל[6c] brings this halocha like Rashi.

---

1. מועד קטן ב: ״מה דרכו של חורש לרפוי ארעא״ 2. רש״י שם ד״ה ״רפוי״ 3. מאירי שבת עג.לרפות את הארץ להיותה ראויה לזריעה. ורש״י שבת עג: ד״ה ״גומא וטממה״ ״הוי רפוי וטוב לזריעה״ 4. מתוך דברי הרמב״ם הל׳ שבת פ״ח הל׳ א. וע׳ באגלי טל חורש סימן ה׳ ס״ק ט׳ ד״ה ״אבל״ 4a. לפי אגלי טל שם וע׳ ירושלמי שבת פ״ז הל׳ ב׳ (דף מז:) ״לכל דבר שהוא להניית קרקע חייב משום חורש״ 5. לפי אגלי טל שם וע׳ ירושלמי שבת פ״ז הלכה ב׳(דף מז:) ״לכל דבר שהוא להניית קרקע חייב משום חורש״ 6. לפי אור זרוע הל׳ שבת ס״ק נ״ה ״החורש״ 6a. שרת פ״ח הל׳ א׳ 6b. כללות שבת כללי ל״ט מלאכות א׳ 6c. חורש סימן ה׳

Avos of חורש(2a)

a) חופר: 7   Digging a hole in the soil to place seeds into it.[8](3)

b) חורץ: 9   Making furrows in the soil.[10]

Toldos of חורש

a) מזבל: 11   (פ״ב מ״ב): Fertilizing the soil.(4)

b) מסקל: 12   (פ״ב מ״ג, פ״ג מ״ז): Removing stones which are embedded in the soil.[13](5)

c) מקרסם: 14   Thinning out grass (עשבים) by plucking up *entire*[15] stalks of good grass from the ground,(6) or[16] cutting dry branches from the moist branches of a tree,(7)

(2a) Concerning Hilchos Shmittoh only those melochos which are specified in the posuk (זורע, זומר, קוצר, בוצר) carry with them the penalty of malkus.[10a]

(3) If the earth is so loose that when one digs a hole it caves in then this is not considered a hole.[8a]

(4) Whether done by hand or machine, see "Shmittoh in General" Chapter Three no. 11.

(5) Those which merely lie on top of the soil may not be removed on account of מראית העין. Those which do not touch the ground one is permitted to remove.[13a]

(6) Which thereby improves the soil[15a] i.e any excess growth drains the soil's strength.[15b] Such thinning out is therefore for the benefit of the soil. It is not for the benefit of the growth of the grass because even without this thinning the grass will grow. i.e one is not thinning the grass because it is overcrowded (compare "המדל" ד״ה in "Toldos of זורע" see footnote (40))

(7) In order that the tree will produce more or better fruit.[16a] This is a Toldah of חורש because as well as ploughing a field before it is sown with seeds where the idea is for making the soil suitable for sowing, there is also ploughing after the field is sown, the idea being to cause the better production of the fruits, i.e. this ploughing is not causing growth but is rather making the existing growth more suitable to produce i.e there is now a better production of fruit, and it is this which is also achieved by being מקרסם. However if one cuts branches from the tree in such a manner that it is in order to cause the very tree itself to grow and become thicker, then this type of מקרסם is a Toldah of זורע.[16b] See "Toldos of זורע" "g".

---

7. שבת עג: עי׳ ברש״י ד״ה ״מלאכה אחת הן״ 8. רש״י שבת מו: ד״ה איסורא דאורייתא״ לפי אגלי טל חורש סימן א׳ ס״ק ב׳ ד״ה ואחד״ 8a. אגלי טל חורש סימן ג׳ 9. שבת עג: עי׳ רש״י ד״ה ״מלאכה אחת הן״ 10. רש״י שם ד״ה ״החורץ״ 10a. רמב״ם שמיטה ויובל פ״א הל׳ ג׳ וריטב״א מועד קטן ג. 11. ירושלמי שבת פ״ז הלכה ב׳ (דף מז:) ורש״י שביעית פ״ב מ״ב 12. ירושלמי שם ורש״ס שם פ״ב מ״ג 13. רש״ס שם פ״ב מ״ג ד״ה ״כאן בתולש כאן במחובר״13a. רש״ס שם. 14. רמב״ם הל׳ שבת פ״ח הל׳ א׳ 15. אגלי טל חורש סימן ה׳ ס״ק ח׳ ד״ה ״והנא הא דבאות״ ״מקרסם עשב אחד כולו״15a. אגלי טל שם. 15b. אגלי טל שם. 16. לפי מאירי שבת קג. ד״ה ״המנכש״16a. אגלי טל שם ד״ה ״והנה בכרת״ 16b. אגלי טל שם.

or[17] hand plucking the kernels of wheat leaving the stalks in the ground as fertilizer.

d) מזרד :[18]   Cutting off even moist branches from a tree.[19(8)]

e) משקה :[20]   Watering a field which is ready to be sown so that the field should be moist during planting.[(9)]

f) מדייר :[21]   (פ"ג מ"ד): Making a sheepfold or cattlepen[(10)] on an area of land thereby fertilizing it with the animal droppings.[22(11)]

g) הבונה מדרגות :[23] Terracing.[(12)]

h) המשוה פני השדה :[24] Flattening out the surface of a field by knocking down mounds which are part of the ground.[25(13)]

i) המשוה גומות :[26] Levelling a field by filling up the holes with earth.

(8) Due to there being too many of them.[19a] This is done in order to improve the soil.[19b] i.e any excess growth drains the soil from its strength. See footnote (6). Or in order that the tree will produce more fruit or better fruit.[19c] See footnote (7) for the reason why this is classified as a Toldah of חורש.

(9) In such a case the water has softened[20a] and improved the soil for sowing.[20b]

(10) From "דייר",[21a] fold or pen.

(11) The animals being brought into the pen for this specific purpose.

(12) This is the shaping of hilly areas of land into the form of steps so that there are stretches of flat land. Thus one has improved the soil making it suitable for sowing.[23a] N.B. This is not the same as "בונין מדרגות על פי הגיאות",[23b] this is building steps on the slopes of valleys in order that people can go down into the valley to draw the water there.[23c] This is forbidden during erev Shviyis because it looks like one is preparing them in order that he will be able to water his field during Shmittoh,[23d] thus it is not a Toldah of חורש.

(13) Removing detached clumps of earth is not considered an act of חורש since the actual ground is already prepared.[25a]

17. הרמב"ם פירוש המשניות שביעית פ"ב מ"ג לפי תורת שביעית שהובא במשנת יוסף תוספות אחרונים ד"ה "מקרסמין" 18. רמב"ם הל' שבת פ"ח הל' א' 19. מאירי שבת קג. ד"ה "המנכש" ורש"י מועד קטן ג. ד"ה "מזרדין" ועי' במשנת יוסף בשיטות המפרשים ד"ה "מזרדין" דאין נפקא מינה אם חותך יבשים או לחים דהעיקר כשחותך ענפים להקל מהאילן היינו מזרדין 19a. מאירי שם ורש"י שם 19b. אגלי טל חורש סימן ה' "המזרד את השריגים כדי ליפות את הקרקע" ורמב"ם שבת פ"ח הל' א' 19c. אגלי טל שם 20. אגלי טל שם סימן ו' 20a. משנה ברורה סימן של"ו ס"ק כ"ו 20b. אגלי טל חורש סימן ו' ושעה"צ סימן של"ו ס"ק י"ח 21. ירושלמי שבת פ"ז הל' ב' (דף מז:) ועי' בכללת שבת "החורש" שזה תולדת חורש 21a. רע"ב 22. רש"ס שם פ"ג מ"ד ופירוש המשניות להרמב"ם 23. על פי אמונת יוסף ירושלמי שביעית פ"ג מ"ח ד"ה "אין בונין מדרגות 23a. על פי אמונת יוסף שם 23b. שביעית פ"ג מ"ח 23c. רש"ס 23d. אמונת יוסף שם 24. שבת עג: "היתה לו גבשושית ונטלה" ועי' רמב"ם הל' שבת פ"ח הל' א' 25. לפי אגלי טל חורש סימן ט' ס"ק י"ד ד"ה "וייראה לי" 25a. אגלי טל שם 26. שבת שם "היתה לו גומא וטממה" ועי' רמב"ם שם

j) מעדר: [27]   (פ״ב מ״ב): Hoeing under vines.[28(14)]

k) מקשקש: Hoeing under olive trees,[29] or[30] stopping up crevices in a tree.[(15)]

l) מנכש: [31]   Removing weeds from healthy grass by plucking up entire stalks of the weeds[32] or from the roots of trees[33(16)] or[34] hoeing around the roots of vines and plants.

m) מכבד: [35]   This is another name for משוה גומות.[36(17)]

n) מפעפע גושים: [37] Breaking clods of earth which are stuck together.[38(18)]

o) ממלא בקעים שתחת הזיתים: [39] Filling in with earth the crevices in the ground[40] under olive trees.[(19)]

(14) When the term "עידור" is used by the Mishna[28a] with regard to מקשאות ומדלעות (gourd and cucumber patches) the Tosfos Yom Tov explains that although עידור generally refers to hoeing under trees, it is borrowed to be used here in connection to gourd and cucumber patches. It is a Toldah of חורש (according to Rashi) because the idea behind it is to soften the earth around the vines.[28b] However the Tosfos Yom Tov here learns that מעדר is the actual melocha of חורש. The Gemora[28c] says that this is permissible during the Shmittoh year. Rashi there explains that this is only in the case where the area has been previously hoed (עתיקי).

(15) This type of מקשקש is permitted during Shmittoh because it is for אוקמי אילנא.[30a]

(16) See footnote (6) for the reason why this is a Toldah of חורש. The difference between מקרסם and מנכש is that concerning מקרסם one is picking the good grass itself, whereas מנכש is picking out the weeds from the good grass.

(17) This speaks of being מכבד in a field, not a house.[36a]

(18) In order to soften them, making them suitable for sowing in them.[38a]

(19) The earth now having the gaps filled has more strength to give greater growth potential to the olive-trees.

28. רש״י מועד קטן ג. ד״ה "עידור" ועי״י "ברש״ס פ״א (דף ח.) ד״ה "אין צ״ל חריש וקציר וכו'". 27
רש״י שם 28a. שביעית פ״ב מ״ב 28b. רש״י שם 28c. מועד קטן שם 29. רש״י מועד קטן שם ד״ה
"יקשקש" 30. מועד קטן שם "סתומי פילי" 30a. מועד קטן שם ורמב״ם שמיטה ויובל פ״א הל' ז'
31. אגלי טל חורש סימן ה' ורמב״ם הל' שבת פ״ח הל' א' 32. רש״י מועד קטן ג. ד״ה כיסוח 33.
אגלי טל שם 34. פירוש המשניות להר״מ שבת פי״ב מ״ב 35. ירושלמי שבת פי״ז הל' ב' (דף מז:) 36.
לפי רבינו חננאל שבת עג: 36a. רבינו חננאל שם 37. ירושלמי שם 38. קרבן העדה בירושלמי שם
ד״ה "המפעפע גושים" 38a. קרבן העדה 39. קרבן העדה שם 40. ירושלמי שם ד״ה "נקעים"

p) עושה עוגיות לגפנים:[41]   Making a hole in the soil around[42] the underneath of a vine.[43(20)]

q) מברה בחרשים:[44] Cutting down small trees in a forest.[45(21)]

r) מצית אור:[46]   Burning down reeds in a field and bad date trees which are in an agam (grassland).[47(22)]

s) עושה את המים:[48] Making canals at the sides of fields.[(23)]

זורע: "Sowing seeds"[49(24)]

Purpose: The idea behind the Av Melocha of זורע is for:

1) צמוחי פירא[50]   Causing plant growth.[(25)]

2) הבחלת פירא[51] Helping the plant to mature[52] or to improve it.[53]

(20) In order to put water in it.[43a] The Gemora[43b] says this melocha is permitted during Shmittoth because it merely prevents loss of the vine (אוקמי אילנא). The reason why it is classified as a Toldah of חורש in Hilchos Shabbos is because making such a hole has not yet prevented this loss, rather one has caused the *earth* to be in a situation where it is now ready to put water in and prevent a loss.

(21) In order that the bigger trees can grow and become thicker.[45a] Being that the Gemora lists it as a Toldah of חורש, then we must say that the small trees are removed in order to relieve the strain on earth which has been too weak to enhance the proper tree growth. See footnote (6).

(22) In order to allow ploughing of the ground which they are standing on.[47a]

(23) This makes the soil suitable for sowing.[48a] However the Rambam[48b] says that during Shmittoh this is permissible.

(24) Inserting something detached into something attached (with regard to plants).[49a]

(25) The term "פירא" here does not only refer to fruit but to the plant in general, because the Gemora here in telling us that the idea behind זורע is for צמוחי פירא refers to how it was in the Mishkon i.e. they used the plants for dyes and not fruit, thus פירא here is used to express all usuable parts of the plant, not merely the fruit.

41. מועד קטן שם וירושלמי שם 42. רש"י מועד קטן ד: ד"ה "עוגיות" 43. רש"י מועד קטן שם 43a. רש"י שם 43b. שם ועיין רמב"ם שמיטה ויובל פ"א הל' ט' 44. ירושלמי שם 45. קרבן העדה 45a. קרבן העדה 46. ירושלמי שם 47. לפי קרבן העדה וגירסת רבינו חננאל שם 47a. קרבן העדה ועי' פני משה 48. ירושלמי שם 48a. ירושלמי שם 48b. שם 49. רש"י שבת עג: ד"ה כולן מלאכה אחת הן 49a. כללות שבת כללי ל"ט מלאכות אב מלאכה 50. מועד קטן ב: "דרכו של זורע לצמוחי פירא" 51. ירושלמי פ"ז הל' ב' (דף מ"ח.) 52. קרבן העדה בירושלמי שם 53. רבינו חננאל שבת עג: בשם הירושלמי שם

Avos of זורע(26)

a) נוטע: [54]		Planting a tree.[55]
b) מבריך: (27)		"Layering" i.e. lowering the branch of a living vine into the ground in a way that the branch can now grow as an independent vine.[56](28)
c) מרכיב:		Grafting trees and plants.

Toldos of זורע

a) זומר: [57](29)		Cutting dry branches from vines.[58]
b) מייבל: [59]	(פ"ב מ"ב)	Cutting off wart-like formations(30) from a tree[60](31) or[61] cutting off dry branches(32) from a tree.

(26) Concerning Hilchos Shmittoh only those melochos which are specified in the posuk (זורע, זומר, קוצר, בוצר) carry with them the penalty of malkus.[53a] Although a melocha like נוטע (planting tree seeds) is not specified in the posuk, nevertheless, as the אגלי טל[53b] mentions, נוטע is the same *action* as זורע differing only in its *name*. Accordingly, it is this *action* which the Torah here is specifically prohibiting and therefore נוטע should also be forbidden midorysa. The Rambam,[53c] however, considers it only prohibited miderabbonon. The אגלי טל suggests that this is because the prohibition of melocha in Shmittoh is only on that which receives *Kedushas Shviyis* (see "Shmittoh in Depth" Chapter Five no. 1). Thus, being that wood receives no *Kedushas Shviyis* then נוטע in Shmittoh is in essence the planting of the *fruit* and not the planting of the tree itself, differing from Shabbos where even the planting of the tree itself is the melocha. Therefore in Shmittoh נוטע, the planting of tree *fruit*, is not done in the ground directly, thereby differing from זורע, and can therefore only be classified as a Toldah.

(27) (לשון "ויברך הגמלים" בראשית כד:יא) referring here to causing the vine to kneel.

(28) For a picture of this see the commentary of the רמב"ם כלאים פ"ז מ"א.

(29) This is considered an Av in Hilchos Shmittoh. See above no. 2.

(30) This is cutting off a יבלת which is a type of formation on a tree similar to that of a wart on a person[59a] and is damaging to a tree.[59b]

(31) After which the tree resumes its normal health.[60a]

(32) Also called "יבולות".

53a. רמב"ם שמיטה ויובל פ"א הל' ג' וריטב"א מועד קטן ג. 53b. זורע סימן א' ס"ק ב' אות ה' 53c. שם הל' ד'. 54. שבת עג. עי' ברש"י ד"ה "כולן מלאכה אחת הן" 55. רש"י שם 56. כלאים פ"ז מ"א 57. שבת עג. עי' רש"י "כולן מלאכה אחת הן" 58. רש"י מועד קטן ג. ד"ה "זימור" 59. רש"ס שביעית פ"ב מ"ב 59a. ר"ש משאנץ לתורת כהנים ריש פרשת בהר ועיין ערוך ערך "יבלת" 59b. ערוך השלחן העתיד סימן י"ט ס"ק ו'. 60. רש"ס פ"ב בגמ' ד"ה מעבירין את היבולת" 60a. רש"ס שם 61. פירוש הרא"ש.

c) מפרק: [62] (פ״ב מ״ב): Removing[33] stones from the roots of a tree[63][34] or[64] removing leaves from a tree.[35]

d) מאבק: [65] (פ״ב מ״ב): Covering exposed roots with dust,[66] or[67] covering the tree itself with dust,[36] or[68] putting a specially prepared powder on the tree trunk,[37] or[69] removing dust from the roots of a tree.

e) מעשן: [70] (פ״ב מ״ב): Making smoke beneath a tree.[71][38]

f) מתליע: Removing insects from a tree[72] by hand[73] or by the use of a sickle or an axe.[74][39]

g) מקרסם: [75] (פ״ב מ״ג): Cutting the top of grass[76][40] (mowing the lawn), or[77] cutting out dry branches from the moist branches of a tree in a manner where it causes the tree itself to grow and become thicker,[41] or[78] cutting off by hand the שבולת[42] and leaving the תבן[43] in the

---

(33) "מפרק" lit. means "unloading".

(34) Which thereby enhances the tree's productivity.[63a]

(35) In order to lighten the load[64a] which is weakening it[64b] or which are overshadowing the fruit and preventing them ripening in the sunlight.[64c]

(36) This could be of potential to help the tree.[67a]

(37) In order to thicken it.[68a]

(38) In order to drive away[71a] or kill insects.[71b]

(39) Some Rishonim[74a] learn that "מתליע" is just another name for the melocha of מעשן.

(40) Cutting off the top of the grass causes the grass to thicken and therefore is a Toldah of זורע. Where entire stalks of grass are uprooted then it is a Toldah of חורש. See "Toldos of חורש "c".

(41) This is the same as "זומר" by vines.[77a] See footnote (7).

(42) These are the kernels on the top part of the wheat-stalk.

(43) Stalk-Stem.[78a]

62. רש״ס פ״ב מ״ב 63. רש״י מועד קטן ג. ד״ה "מפרקין" 63a. ר״ש משאנץ שם בלשון אחר 64. רמב״ם פירוש המשניות ור״ש פ״ב מ״ב 64a. רמב״ם ור״ש שם 64b. ר״ש משאנץ לתו״כ שם 64c. תוס' הרא״ש מועד קטן ג. 65. רש״ס שם 66. רש״י מועד קטן ג. ד״ה "מאבקין" 67. פירוש המשניות לר״מ. ועי' בשושנים לדוד ופאת השולחן סי' א' ס״ק ט' דשיטות רש״י ורמב״ם חלוקות הן. 67a. פיה״מ לר״מ שם. 68. ראב״ד לתו״כ ריש פרשת בהר 68a. ראב״ד שם 69. ערוך ערך "אבק" 70. רש״ס שם 71. רש״י מועד קטן ג. ד״ה "מעשנין" 71a. רש״י שם 71b. רש״י שם 72. רש״י ע״ז נ: ד״ה "מתליעין" 73. חזו״א שביעית סי' י״ז ס״ק י״ט סוף ד״ה "שם מדרבנן" 74. רבינו חננאל ע״ז נ: 74a. רש״ס פ״ב גמ' על מ״ד ועיין בהמרכבת המשנה הל' יום טוב פ״ח הל' י' 75. ירושלמי שבת פ״ז הל' ב' (דף מח.). 76. אגלי טל שם ד״ה חורש סימן ה' ס״ק ח' ד״ה "והנה הא דבאות" "שכורת מקצת מן העשד למעלה" 77. אגלי טל שם ד״ה "והנה בכרת ועי' רש״י מועד קטן ג. ד״ה "מקרסמין" 77a. רש״י מועד קטן שם ד״ה מקרסמין 78. רמב״ם פירוש המשניות שביעית פ״ב מ״ג 78a. עיין תוי״ט בבא מציעא פ״ט מ״א ד״ה "בתבן"

ground,[44] or[79] cutting off the tops of vegetables.[45]

h) מזרד [80]   (פ״ב מ״ג): Cutting off even moist branches as well as dry branches from a tree.[81][46]

i) מפסל [82]   (פ״ב מ״ג): Cutting off *all* the branches of the tree.[83][47]

j) מפסג [48]   Tying up branches which have become spread out, so that they now point upwards and are no longer a burden on the body of the tree.[84]

k) מזהם [85]   (פ״ב מ״ד): Applying fertilizer to the parts of a tree[86] where the bark has fallen off due to disease,[87][49] or[88] anointing a tree with זהומא, a foul-smelling oil.[89][50]

---

(44) Unloading the stem from excess kernels in order that all the kernels do not break off on account of their heaviness before they have ripened. If they fall off before ripening then they will dry out. Therefore מקרסם by grain is the same as מזרד by trees. If one cuts the kernels off after they have ripened then it comes under the melocha of קוצר (reaping grain and legumes) which if done by hand is a שינוי and permitted, therefore the Mishna in speaking of a prohibition speaks about cutting kernels before they ripen which is prohibited on account of מקרסם.[78b]

(45) For the purpose of bettering the growth of the vegetable. If it is cut for food then it is the melocha of קוצר.

(46) Due to there being too many of them. [81a] Thinning the tree from the branches lightens the burden of the tree[81b] so that the tree will grow and become thicker. See end of footnote.(7)

(47) In order that its trunk should grow thicker.[83a]

(48) Some Rishonim[83b] use this word instead of "מפסל".

(49) By doing this it can either prevent the tree from dying (אוקמי אילנא)[87a] or it can improve the tree and make it healthier (i.e "אברויי אילנא" i.e. there are two types of זיהום.[87b]

(50) The smell of which keeps worms away from it and prevents birds pecking it when soft.[89a] This is different from מעשן (see "e") because מעשן is not something which is being done on the actual body of the tree.[89b]

78b. לפי תורת שביעית הובא במשנת יוסף תוספות אחרונים ד״ה "מקרסמין" 79. פירוש המשניות
להרמב״ם שבת פ״ב מ״ב 80. ירושלמי שם 81. רש״י מועד קטן ג ד״ה "מזרדין" ומאירי שבת קג.
ד״ה "המנכש" 81a. רש״י ומאירי שם 81b. רש״י שם 82. ירושלמי שם 83. רש״ס פ״ב מ״ג והיש
אומרים שהובא ברא״ש ובר׳ו ור״ש ולא כפירוש הראשון שלהם דהיינו מקרסם (רש״ס) 83a.
רש״ס שם והיש אומרים שם 83b. רש״י מועד קטן ג. ומנוקי יוסף שם ברישא ד״ה "משקין" 84.
נמוקי יוסף שם 85. ירושלמי שם 86. לפי משנה ראשונה פ״ב מ״ד ד״ה "את הנטיעות" דלאו דוקא
נטיעות 87. רש״י עבודה זרה נ: ד״ה "ומזהמין" 87a. רש״י שם 87b. עי׳ גמ׳ עבודה זרה שם 88. ר״מ
פירוש המשניות שביעית פ״ב מ״ד 89. ר״מ פיה״מ שם 89a. ר״מ שם רמב״ם שמיטה ויובל פ״א הל׳ ה׳ 89b.
תוי״ט שביעית פ״ב מ״ד ד״ה "מזהמין"

l) כורך [90] (פ״ב מ״ד): Tying together the ends of the branches of a tree so that they do not sag to the ground,[91(51)] or[92] tying leaves around a sapling to prevent it from drying out or[93] tying rags[94] around a sapling to protect it from the sun or the cold.

m) קוטם [95] (פ״ב מ״ד): Cutting off the *ends*[96] of branches,[97(52)] or[98] putting ash onto the roots of the tree,[99(53)] or[100] putting ash onto the branches of the tree.[(54)]

n) עושה בתים [101] (פ״ב מ״ב): Putting a fence one אמה[(55)] high around a tree[102] and filling it up with earth,[103(56)] or[104] making an actual house or shade around the entire height of the tree,[(57)] or[105] digging crevices among the roots of the tree.[(58)]

o) משקה [106] (פ״ב מ״ד): Any kind of watering to a tree[107] or a sown field,[108] or[109] heavy watering in an orchard where the trees are spread far apart from one another.

(51) This is like מפסג. See "j".

(52) In order that many branches will sprout out around the trunk of the tree[97a] another name for this is "מגזם".[97b]

(53) Unlike מאבק (see "d") which is putting ash onto the branches.[99a]

(54) Unlike מאבק which is putting ash onto the roots.[100a]

(55) According to the איש חזון this is 57.6cm. According to ר׳ חיים נאה this is 48cm.

(56) The rain will go into this earth[103a] and the tree will thereby receive extra nourishment.

(57) This protects it from the sun and the cold.[104a]

(58) So the rain will gather in them and water them.[105a]

90. רש״ס פ״ב מ״ד. 91. ר״מ פיה״מ שם. 92. מהר״י בן מלכי צדק שביעית פ״ב מ״ד. 93. רש״ס שם. 94. תפארת ישראל אות כ״ז. 95. רש״ס שם. 96. ע׳ במלאכת שלמה. לפיכך אין זה מזרד או מפסל או זומר. 97. פירוש הרא״ש ורש״ס ור״מ פיה״מ. ע״פ משנת יוסף בשיטת המפרשים. 97a רש״י עבודה זרה נ: ד״ה "כאן וכאן" 97b. רש״ס. 98. רש״ס. 99. הערוך. 99. רש״ס בשם הר״מ הל׳ שמיטה ויובל פ״א הל׳ ה׳. 99a רש״ס בשם רמב״ן שם. 100. רש״ס בשם רש״י. 100a רש״ס שם. 101. רש״ס שם. 102. לפי משנה ראשונה שאין חילוק בין נטיעה לאילן ומהמשמעות הרע״ב. 103. רש״י שם ד״ה "ועושין להם בתים" ופירוש הרא״ש בשביעית. 103a שנות אליהו. 104. רא״ש בשם הירושלמי ופיה״מ להר״מ. 104a רש״ס ופיה״מ להר״ם שם. 105. רבינו חננאל עבודה זרה נ: 105a. רבינו חננאל שם. 106. רש״ס פ״ב מ״ד. 107. ע׳ משנה ראשונה לפי פשט הראשון. 108. ע׳ משנה ברורה סי׳ של״ז ס״ק כ״ו ושער הציון ס״ק י״ח ועי׳ ברש״ס ד״ה "מרביצין בעפר לבן" 109. משנה ראשונה לפי פשט השני

p) ‏סך:‏[110]   (‏פ״ב מ״ה‏): Smearing unripe figs or other unripe fruit[111] with oil.[59]

q) ‏מנקב‏[112]:   (‏פ״ב מ״ה‏): Puncturing unripe figs or other unripe fruit in order to put oil into them or for the rain to penetrate them.[60]

r) ‏הרבצה‏:   (‏פ״ב מ״י‏): Any kind of watering to a grain field,[113(61)] or[114] light watering in an orchard where the trees are spread far apart from one another.[62]

s) ‏ממרס‏:   (‏פ״ב מ״י‏): Watering a rice field.[63]

t) ‏מכסח‏:   (‏פ״ב מ״י‏): Cutting leaves from the rice,[115(64)] or[116] cutting the tops of weeds to enhance the growth of the good grass.[65]

u) ‏מנכש‏:   Removing bad grass from good grass by plucking up entire stalks.[117(66)]

(59) In order to hasten their ripening [111a] or just to make them more succulent.[111b]

(60) So that they ripen more quickly[112a] or become more succulent.[112b]

(61) According to one Tanna[113a] (‏רבי אליעזר בן יעקב‏) this is a forbidden melocha.

(62) See footnote (61).

(63) This watering is referred to as "‏ממרס‏" because it requires such a large amount of water that the soil mixes with the water.[114a] Without such watering there is a complete crop loss, therefore it is permitted during Shmittoh.[114b]

(64) This is the same as pruning of vines.[115a](65) This is unlike ‏מקרסם‏ (see "g") which is cutting the top of good grass for the benefit of the good grass.

(66) In order for the good grass to benefit. According to footnote (40) this might only be a Toldah of ‏חורש‏, however this is unlike ‏מקרסם‏, a Toldah of ‏חורש‏, because there entire stalks of *good* grass are plucked whereas here it involves weeding entire stalks of *bad* grass which is more likely being done for the benefit of the good grass, it thus being the Toldah of ‏זורע‏. On the other hand, ‏מנכש‏ is also a Toldah of ‏חורש‏. See footnote (16).

110. ‏רש״ס פ״ב מ״ה‏ 111. ‏משמעות הרע״ב ע״י במשנת יוסף תוספות אחרותים‏ 111a. ‏רש״ס ופירוש הרא״ש ור״מ פיה״מ‏ b‏111.רש״י עבודה זרה נ:‏ 112. ‏רש״ס שם‏ 112a. ‏פירוש הרא״ש‏ b‏112. רש״ס בשם רש״י עבודה זרה נ:‏ 113. ‏ע״י משנה ראשונה שביעית פ״ב מ״ד ד״ה ״ומשקין״ לפי פשט הראשון והרע״ב בפ״ב מ״י‏ 113a. ‏שביעית פ״ב מ״י‏ 114. ‏משנה ראשונה לפי פשט השני וע״י בפיה״מ להר״מ ד״ה ״מרביצין״‏ 114a. ‏רש״ס‏ b‏114. ‏תפארת ישראל אות ע׳‏ 115. ‏פירוש הרא״ש ורש״ס‏ 115a. ‏פירוש הרא״ש ורש״ס‏ 116. ‏רש״י מועד קטן ג. ד״ה ״כיסוח״‏ 117. ‏רש״י שם‏

v) המדל: (פ"ד מ"ד): Uprooting one or two of every three[118] olive or vine[119] saplings.[67]

w) מחפה בעפר (פ"ד מ"ה): Filling in with earth the crevices in a tree.[120][68]

x) הקוצץ בתולת שקמה (פ"ד מ"ה): Cutting a sycamore tree's branches for the first time.[69]

y) מזנב בגפנים (פ"ד מ"ו): Cutting off the tails of vines.[70]

z) הקוצץ קנים (פ"ד מ"ו): Cutting reeds.[71]

z^a) חורש: Ploughing in order to cover over seeds which have been sown.[121][72]

(67) When young olive trees or vines grow too close to each other then one uproots them in the way mentioned so that the remaining saplings can grow and thicken.[119a] We find that the Mishna here permits this melocha even according to Bais Hillel who learn that it is permissible to uproot the entire root (ישרש). The question is why it is not prohibited like מפסל ומזדר since it enhances growth? The Tosfos Yom Tov answers that the case in the Mishna here is where it is only done because the person wants the wood, however the question remains that it should still be prohibited since it is a פסיק רישא that the action helps the growth of the saplings.[119b]

(68) The earth becomes like cement and improves the tree.[120a]

(69) This improves the tree[120b] and strengthens it for its production of the fruit[120c] and this is the same as זומר of vines.[120d]

(70) For the purpose of causing the stems of the vines to thicken and strengthen.[120e] Accordingly this is a form of זומר.[120f] However other Rishonim[120g] learn that this is not a form of זומר because זומר is cutting off entire branches whereas מזנב is just cutting off the ends[120h] and thereby lightening the burden of weight on the vine so that it does not dry out.[120i] This is permissible according to the Mishna only because it speaks of where one wants the wood for fire,[120j] and such cutting is not a melocha of קוצר. See "Shmittoh in General" no. 6.

(71) So that they should grow taller.[120k] This is permissible according to the Mishna for the reason mentioned in footnote (70).

(72) The idea behind such ploughing is to help the growth of what has already begun to grow, thus a Toldah of זורע.[121a] Thus such חורש done during Shmittoh certainly is a Toldah falling under the negative prohibition of"שדך לא תזרע".[121b] Ploughing done in order to prepare the soil for sowing, helps the soil and not any existing growth. Therefore it is not a Toldah of זורע but a melocha in its own right.

---

118. רש"ס שביעית פ"ד מ"ד ורע"ב שם 119. עי' פאה פ"ז מ"ה 119a. רש"ס ורע"ב שם ורש"י מועד קטן ד: "המדל" 119b. עיין במשנת יוסף ד"ה "המדל בזיתים" 120. עי' תוספתא שביעית פ"ג אות י' עם פירוש חסידי דוד דכל האילנות בכלל זה. 120a. ירושלמי שביעית פ"ס הל' ג' ועיין רש"ס ד"ה "לא יכסה בעפר" 120b. רש"ס 120c. פיה"מ לר"מ 120d. רש"ס ופירוש הרא"ש ורע"ב 120e. רש"ס ופירוש הרא"ש ורע"ב 120f. עיין משנה ראשונה 120g. הערוך ורמב"ם עיין משנה ראשונה 120h. משנה ראשונה 120i. משנה ראשונה 120j. רש"ס 120k. פירוש הרא"ש ורש"ס 121. רש"י שם פסחים מז: 121a. עיין מכות פ"ג מ"ט ורש"י פסחים שם 121b. רש"י שם

קוצר: reaping grain and legumes.[122]

Purpose: The idea behind the Av Melocha of קוצר is to עוקר דבר מגידולו[123] to detach a product from its source of growth.

Avos of קוצר[(73)]

a) בוצר: [124(74)] Picking grapes[125]

b) גודר: [126]   Picking dates[127]

c) מוסק: [128]   Picking olives[129]

d) אורה: [130]   Picking figs[131]

Toldos of קוצר

a) תולש[132]   Picking produce by hand[133(75)] if it is not the normal way to pick this produce by hand.[134(76)]

b) מנענע: [135]   Shaking a tree so that the fruit falls from it.

---

(73) Concerning Hilchos Shmittoh only those melochos which are specified in the posuk (זורע, זומר, קוצר, בוצר) carry with them the penalty of malkus.[123a]

(74) Tosfos[124a] understands that בוצר in Hilchos Shmittoh is a Toldah.

(75) Unlike the Avos of קוצר which are picking with the use of an instrument.[133a] This makes it two different types of action; when one picks produce by hand he is plucking it up, but when he picks it with the use of an instrument he is cutting it. However the idea behind both actions is the same (detaching a plant from its source of growth). One will notice that even though the idea behind the actions is the same nevertheless the Rambam still classifies תולש as a Toldah. This appears to be contradictory to the way the אגלי טל[133b] learns.

(76) For instance, the fixed way of reaping wheat is to detach it by use of an instrument. Therefore if one picks wheat by hand it is a Toldah of קוצר, picking it by hand is not considered כלאחר יד (deviation) that it should be considered exempt, rather it is just not the fixed way of reaping the wheat. However reaping with an instrument is always considered and Av melocha even though it is not the fixed way.[134a] e.g. the fixed way of reaping cotton is by hand, if it is done by instrument it remains an Av Melocha.

---

122. רמב"ם הל' שבת פ"ז הל' ד'. 123. שבת ק"ז. 123a: רמב"ם שמיטה ויובל כ"א הל' ג' ורימב"א מועד קטן ג'. 124. שבת עג: 124a: בבא מציעא נח. ד"ה "לשמור" 125. רמב"ם הל' שבת פ"ז הל' ד' 126. שבת שם 127. רש"י שבת עג: ד"ה "גודר" ורמב"ם שם 128. שבת שם 129. רש"י שם ד"ה "ומוסק" ורמב"ם שם 130. שבת שם 131. רש"י שם ד"ה "אורה" ורמב"ם שם 132. רמב"ם הל' שבת פ"ח הל' ג' רש"י שבת עג: ד"ה "תולש" 133. לחם משנה שם ועי' רש"י חולין קלז. ד"ה "תולש" 133a. לחם משנה שם ורש"י שם 133b: זורע סימן א' ס"ק ב' אות ו' ד"ה "אך" 134. אגלי טל קוצר סימן א' ס"ק ג' וסימן ה' ס"ק י"ג 134a. אגלי טל שם 135. על פי אגלי טל קוצר סימן ו' על פי ירושלמי ביצה פ"ה הל' ב'

CHAPTER FOUR

TOSEFES SHVIYIS

1. Deriving the source of Tosefes Shviyis

There is a dispute between Rabbi Akiva and Rabbi Yishmoel regarding from where the halocha of Tosefes Shviyis is derived.[1]

Rabbi Akiva

The Torah[2] says ״ששת ימים תעבד וביום השביעי תשבת בחריש ובקציר תשבת״ "Six days you shall work but on the seventh day you shall rest, (from involvement) in ploughing and reaping you shall rest". Should this posuk be referring to Shabbos, as its simple meaning would imply, it would seem to be redundant, for the Torah[3] already says ״ששת ימים תעבוד ועשית כל מלאכתך ויום השביעי שבת וגו׳״ "six days you shall work and the seventh day rest etc". Rabbi Akiva solves this problem by saying that this seeming redundancy[4] of the posuk tells us of a prohibition to plough and reap produce at a different time, not Shabbos.

When is this other time?

If we say that the prohibition mentioned in the posuk is to apply during the Shmittoh year[(1)] then it would still be seemingly redundant, for the Torah has already commanded us elsewhere[5] with[6] ״שש שנים תזרע...שדך לא תזרע...את ספיח קצירך לא תקצור״ "six years you shall sow...your field you shall not sow...the s'fiach[(2)] you shall

---

(1) The words ״ששת ימים״ can mean ״שש שנים״ as we find the Torah says elsewhere[4a] ״ימים או עשור״. The word ״ימים״ here is interpreted to mean "a year"[4b].

(2) See Chapter Six.

---

1. ירושלמי שביעית פרק א׳ ריש הלכה א׳ 2. שמות לד: כא 3. שמות כ: ט״י 4. עי׳ תוס׳ רע״ק שביעית אות ג׳ 4a. בראשית כד: נה 4b. רש״י על הפסוק, ורש״ס שביעית פ״א הל׳ א ד״ה ״ואם לענין שבתות שנים״ 5. ויקרא כה:ג 6. לפי גירסת גמ׳ בבלי ראש השנה ט. ומועד קטן ג׳ ועי׳ תוס׳ מועד קטן שם ריש ד״ה ״שהרי״

not reap".[3] The posuk "ששת ימים...בחריש ובקציר תשבות" is therefore telling us neither about a prohibition of ploughing or reaping produce *during* Shabbos or *during* Shmittoh, it must be telling us that this prohibition applies either *before* the commencement of one of these two times, or *after* they have ended. The Gemora[7] says that it tells us that the prohibition of ploughing is to commence sometime before the Shmittoh year,[4][5][6] and the prohibition of reaping produce extends for sometime after the Shmittoh year has ended.

From the above we can now gain a clear understanding of the posuk "בחריש ובקציר תשבות" "(from involvement) in ploughing and

---

(3) We therefore see that reaping produce during Shmittoh has been forbidden here. As far as חורש is concerned, see footnote (6).

(4) The Torah here left it for the Chachomim to decide how long this pre-Shmittoh prohibition should be for.[7a] They decided on a thirty day period.[7b]

(5) It should seem more likely to be telling us that there is a prohibition before Shabbos since the posuk here speaks of Shabbos and not Shmittoh. This remains a question to some.[7c] Others try to answer it.[7d]

(6) The posuk of "את ספיח קצירך לא תקצר" only mentions a prohibiton of reaping and not of ploughing. This would mean that the "בחריש" of "בחריש ובקציר" is not extra that we must derive from it a prohibition of חורש *before* Shmittoh but rather only derive from it the prohibition *during* Shmittoh. However, since בחריש is in juxtaposition with "ובקציר" by way of *hekesh* we can compare חריש to קציר and just as there is a halocha of Tosefes Shviyis with regard to reaping so it applies to ploughing.[7e] It is also possible that "בחריש" is after all redundant since there is already a כלל ופרט וכלל (see Chapter Three "Shmittoh in Depth" no. 2) which tells us that חורש is forbidden during Shmittoh. Thus "בחריש" must be revealing that חורש is prohibited *before* the Shmittoh year.[7f] Although the כלל ופרט וכלל tells us a negative commandment against חורש during Shmittoh we cannot assume that "בחריש" consequently tells us there is also a positive commandment against חורש since in such a case rather than telling us a second prohibition the Torah is usually coming to tell us a new halocha as in the case here (Tosefes Shviyis). Only where we find that no new halocha can be learned from the posuk must we say that it is to tell us that one transgresses two commandments, one negative and one positive.

---

7. ירושלמי שם ומועד קטן שם 7a. תוס׳ מועד קטן ד. ד״ה ״אלא״ (קמא) ועיין בחזו״א שביעית סימן י״ז ס״ק י״ב 7b. עיין רש״ס שם ד״ה ״לא יסור שני פרקים״ 7c. תוס׳ רע״ק שביעית אות ג׳ 7d. עיין משנה ראשונה שביעית פ״א מ״ד ד״ה ״אין״ 7e. לפי תוס׳ מועד קטן ג: ד״ה ״שהרי״ בתירץ ראשון וז״ל לההיא דרשא לאתיא קצירה אתיא חרישה 7f. לפי תירץ שני בתוס׳ שם.

in reaping you shall rest." The Torah here is telling us:[8]

1) "תשבות...בחריש" "(from involvement) in ploughing (where the produce resulting from this ploughing will be forbidden to reap [ובקציר]) you shall rest". The only reaping expressly forbidden in the Torah is reaping done during Shmittoh itself.[7] The only ploughing leading to such reaping is ploughing done before Shmittoh. Thus, the Torah here has forbidden ploughing even before Shmittoh.

2) "...ובקציר תשבות" "and (from involvement) in reaping of produce (which grew at a time when ploughing [בחריש] was forbidden) you shall rest". Only during Shmittoh does the Torah expressly prohibit ploughing.[8] The crop resulting is ready for reaping after Shmittoh. Thus the Torah here has expressed that the reaping of any produce stemming from the Shmittoh year is forbidden to be reaped.[9][10] This completes Rabbi Akiva's understanding of the posuk.[9]

Rabbi Yishmoel

Rabbi Yishmoel[10] understands that the posuk "ששת ימים...בחריש ובקציר תשבות" can in fact speak of Shabbos as its simple meaning implies. As far as its seeming redundancy (see above) is concerned, then this is solved by understanding that the posuk is telling us a special din, that the omer[11] may be reaped on Shabbos. The posuk mentions that one must rest from ploughing on Shabbos,

---

(7) The commandment "לא תקצור".

(8) Such as from the positive commandment "ושבתה הארץ". See Chapter Three.

(9) The Bartenora[8a] explains how it is possible to have produce ready for reaping after Shmittoh if it is forbidden to sow during Shmittoh, i.e. either the produce is s'fichim (that which grows without man having intentionally sown it, see Chapter Six) or one transgressed and sowed during Shmittoh.

(10) Meaning in the usual fashion. However it is permitted to reap it with a deviation just like during Shmittoh.[8b] (see Chapter Seven).

(11) The offering brought in the Mikdosh from the new barley harvest, after which the new crop is permitted for general use.

---

8. ר"ש שביעית פ"א מ"א ועי' מועד קטן ג:ד. 8a. שביעית פ"א מ"ד b8. תוס' ראש השנה ט. ד"ה "וקציר" (בתרא) 9. מועד קטן ג: ראש השנה ט. 10.שביעית פ"א מ"ד ובמועד קטן ד.

(בחריש...תשבות) and reaping is compared to ploughing, that just as there is no instance when ploughing is a mitzvoh, and the Torah's prohibition refers therefore only to optional ploughing, so too the only reaping which the Torah prohibits on Shabbos is similarly optional reaping. The reaping of the omer, a mitzvoh, is therefore permitted on Shabbos. The posuk therefore in no way refers to Tosefes Shviyis, which Rabbi Yishmoel says is a הלכה למשה מסיני.

Rabbi Nechunya, also had the tradition that Tosefes Shviyis is a הלכה למשה מסיני as he stated:[11] "If ten saplings are growing in an orchard and they are equally distributed within an area a size of a *Bais Se'oh*,[12] it is a הלכה למשה מסיני that the whole *Bais Se'oh* may be ploughed for their benefit right up until Rosh Hashona of the Shmittoh year."[13][14] From the fact that a special הלכה למשה מסיני is needed to permit ploughing for the benefit of saplings until Rosh Hashona then this הלכה למשה מסיני is also informing us that there is a prohibition to plough for the benefit of any trees which do *not* come within the category of "sapling"[12][15]. Thus the halocha of Tosefes

---

(12) This is the name given to an area of land which is large enough to have one se'oh (approx. 14.4 litre[11a]) of wheat grown in it[11b] this being an area of 50 by 50 אמות (one אמה being either 57.6cm [חזו״א] or 48cm ([הגרא״ח נאה]. The courtyard of the Mikdosh was 50 x 100 אמה (twice the area of a בית סאה) and it was termed as being בית סאתים[11c,] hence half that area is called a *"Bais Se'oh"*.

(13) The Torah here is lenient in order to prevent one from a financial loss being that saplings can quickly dry out and die from a lack of ploughing.[11d]We therefore have been taught two things from this הלכה למשה מסיני.[11e] 1) It is permitted to plough until Rosh Hashona in order to save the loss of saplings 2) by having given us the measurement of ten to a *Bais Se'oh* then we understand that what is considered ploughing that saves a loss is if it is done within the distance from which they draw their nourishment (יניקה) because the יניקה of ten saplings equally spread out in a *Bais Se'oh* covers the whole area of the *Bais Se'oh*. Therefore one may also plough the distance of the יניקה of just one sapling standing by itself.[11f]

(14) For the intricate details see the Mishnayos.[11g]

(15) There is a dispute amongst the Tannoim concerning until when a tree is still considered a sapling.[12a]

11.מועד קטן ג: 11a. ע״פ חזו״א קונטרס השעורים 11b. רע״ב כלאים פ״ב מ״ב 11c. רש״י בבא בתרא כו: ד״ה ״עשר נטיעות״ 11d. ר״ש שביעית פ״א מ״ו 11e. על פי רש״י סוכה לד. ד״ה ״עשר נטיעות״ ורש״ש 11f. רש״י שם 11g. שביעית פ״א מ״ו-ח׳ 12 תוס׳ מועד קטן ג: ד״ה ״הלכה״ 12a. שביעית פ״א מ״ח

Shviyis has been inferred from this הלכה למשה מסיני. The Gemora goes on and brings the statement of Rabbi Yitzchok that this הלכה למשה מסיני also tells us that Tosefes Shviyis begins thirty days before Rosh Hashona of the Shmittoh year.

Rabbi Akiva learns that there was no such הלכה למשה מסיני and that the halocha of Tosefes Shviyis is learned from the posuk of "בחריש ובקציר תשבות" as brought above.(16)

Some Rishonim13 explain that the only melocha forbidden before Shmittoh which is derived from בחריש ובקציר תשבות is חורש, it being the only melocha specified for this in the posuk(17) (the mention of קוצר is for Motzoai Shmittoh). Although a Mishna14 specifies the melochos נוטע (planting trees), מבריך (layering vines) and מרכיב (grafting onto trees) as also being forbidden thirty days before Shmittoh, this is not on account of the din midorysa of Tosefes Shviyis but is a תקנה דרבנן to avoid מראית העין.15(18) Other Rishonim,16 however, dispute this and explain that in all probability(19) the posuk here teaches us that as well as חורש being forbidden during Tosefes Shviyis so are other melochos(20) forbidden.(21)(22)

(16) Accordingly it is only Rabbi Akiva who learns that there is a prohibition of reaping after the close of the Shmittoh year.
(17) The same being true for the הלכה למשה מסיני of Rabbi Yishmoel.
(18) See below no. 4. According to these Rishonim this was even in the time of the Mikdosh when Tosefes Shviyis was midorysa, see footnote (37).
(19) See footnote (22) for the reasoning behind such a probability.
(20) The melochos זורע, זומר, קוצר, בוצר which are written clearly in the Torah.16a This, therefore, excludes all other melochos even if they are understood to be forbidden midorysa during Shmittoh, since they are learned to be midorysa only from a drosha such as that of the Bnei haYeshiva (see Chapter Three "Shmittoh in Depth" no. 2) or from the general prohibition of "ושבתה הארץ".16b Concerning melochos which are forbidden miderabbonon such as Toldos (see ibid), they are permitted during Tosefes Shviyis. See here "Shmittoh in General" no. 2.
(21) The same being true for the הלכה למשה מסיני of Rabbi Yishmoel.
(22) Rather than the posuk teaching that Tosefes Shviyis is limited only to חורש it is

13. רבינו תם בתוס' ראש השנה ט: ד"ה "ומותר" לפי תירץ ראשון 14. לפי תירץ ראשון פ"ב מ"ו 15. תוס' ראש השנה ט: ד"ה "ומותר" וע"ע בתוי"ט שם ריש ד"ה "פחות" 16. תוס' הרא"ש על תוס' ראש השנה שם. וכן המשמעות מהר"ש שביעית פ"ב מ"ב ד"ה "מעדרין" ועיין ברע"ק אות ט"ו, ותוס' עבודה זרה נ: ד"ה "ומשקין" 16a. חזו"א שביעית סימן י"ז ס"ק י"ח על תוס' עבודה זרה נ: ד"ה "ומשקין" 16b. חזו"א שם

2. Tosefes Shviyis for Ploughing. (Bais Shammai and Bais Hillel)[17]

During the period of the Second Bais haMikdosh Bais Shammai and Bais Hillel instituted Tosefes Shviyis for ploughing even earlier than thirty days before Rosh Hashona of the Shmittoh year.[23] This was *not* an extension to the din dorysa of Tosefes Shviyis[24] (which as seen above was a הלכה למשה מסיני or גזרת הכתוב giving no specific reason) but rather they were concerned that by permitting ploughing so close to Shmittoh (i.e until thirty days before Rosh Hashona) it would lead to ploughing during Shmittoh itself. Why is this? Since[18] ploughing thirty days before Shmittoh appears to benefit the land during Shmittoh itself the farmer may assume "if it is beneficial for Shmittoh and yet it is permitted, then what difference does it make if it is done now or during Shmittoh, it is anyway all for the Shmittoh year, therefore it must actually be permitted to plough during Shmittoh itself."

When does this extended period of Tosefes Shviyis begin?

This is dependent on what type of field one wants to plough, an orchard (שדה אילן) or a grain field (שדה לבן).

more probable that it reveals that Tosefes Shviyis applies to all melochos forbidden by the Torah during Shmittoh. The posuk in mentioning חורש is therefore just an example (by the fact that it tells us that חורש is forbidden during Tosefes Shviyis then it is clearly telling us that חורש is forbidden during Shmittoh itself.[16c] This reasoning could also be applied if Tosefes Shviyis is a הלכה למשה מסיני.

(23) The reason why they only instituted an extended period for the melocha of חורש as opposed to other melochos is explained below.

(24) This is according to the understanding of the Tiferes Yisroel.[17a] According to the Bartenora in one place[17b] he states that the Torah gave a commandment of Tosefes Shviyis and Bais Shammai and Bais Hillel estimated how long this period should be therefore their stated periods are the periods midorysa.[17c] However in another place[17d] he understands that they themselves instituted an additional period of time to the period of Tosefes Shviyis midorysa (similar to the Tiferes Yisroel). This contradiction in the Bartenora remains a difficulty.[17e]

16c. חזו"א שם ס"ק א' ד"ה "מיהו" 17. מועד קטן ג':ד. לפי פירוש ת"י שביעית ס"ק ג' 17a. שם
17b. שביעית פ"א מ"ד 17c. עיין משנה ראשונה פ"א רי"ש ד"ה "ערב שביעית" 17d. שם מ"א
ד"ה "עד העצרת" 17e. משנה ראשונה שם 18. לפי הרע"ב שביעית פ"א מ"א "ומן העצרת ואילך
נראה כמתקן לצורך שביעית" ועי' בתירוץ שני בתוס' ר"ה ט: ד"ה "ומותר"

The prohibition in a grain field begins from the Pesach preceding the Shmittoh year.[19] Until such a date[20] most of the moisture from the winter rains is still in the soil. Any ploughing done before this time is clearly seen to be for the purpose of sowing and producing growth during the sixth year. Therefore the aforementioned confusion will not occur. However, after Pesach the soil is already drying out, not the optimal time for sowing crops. Ploughing at such a time cannot be said to be being done for sixth year produce and will appear to be ploughing for the benefit of Shmittoh and could cause the confusion mentioned above.

Concerning an area in which trees are growing, then if there are three trees equally distributed[(24a)] within a *Bais Se'oh*[(25)] and are capable[21] of producing a minimum crop (calculated by viewing the tree as though it were a fig tree and could produce in one year,[22] a crop of figs sufficient to make a fig loaf weighing a מנה באיטלקי[(26)]) then this area of *Bais Se'oh* is considered an orchard (שדה אילן), the

---

(24a) For measurements see below no. 6.

(25) For details of *Bais Se'oh* see footnote (12). For details of the distribution of the trees see below no. 6.

(26) Sixty *monna* in weight, according to the *monna* of the city Italky. Italky (also referred to as "Italia"[22a]) was the name of a large city in Greece. When the Romans conquered the Greek Empire the city became theirs.[22b] Therefore Italky is referred to as a "great city of Rome".[22c] The weight מנה which was in Italky is referred to as "מנה באיטלקי". The weight of a מנה באיטלקי is equal to the weight of 100 דינרים, a דינר weighing 6 מעות, and a מעה weighing 16 average-size barley seeds.[22d] Since the weight of 20 barley seeds is estimated to be one gram[22e] then one מנה weighs 480 grams, sixty מנה weighing 28.8 kilograms. A reason for this requirement[22f] is that since the branches of these trees are big enough in size to produce such an amount of fruit, therefore the whole *Bais Se'oh* is required for the trees. The reason why מנה באיטלקי is used as the standard is because it was a standard weight at the time the Torah was given[22g] therefore when Chazal wanted to express any measurement they felt it befitting to express them according to the standard measurement of the Torah.

---

19. שביעית פ״ב מ״א 20. לפי ירושלמי על המשנה שם ועיין ברע״ב 21. ערוך השלחן העתיד הל׳ שמיטה ויובל סימן י״ח ס״ק ט׳ והלכתא גבירתא 22. ירושלמי שביעית פ״א הל׳ ג׳ 22a. ערוך 22b. רש״י שבת נו: ד״ה "איטליאה" 22c. שבת שם ומגילה ו: 22d. רע״ב שביעית פ״א מ״ב 22e. שיעורין של תורה סימן שיעור המצות ס״ק ט״ו 22f. רש״ס עיין משנת יוסף עמוד מ׳ ס״ק ג׳ וערוך השלחן העתיד סימן י״ח ס״ק ט׳ 22g. רש״י ורע״ב שם וערוך

whole of which may be ploughed[27] even after Pesach.[23] This is because,[24] unlike in a grain field, ploughing done in an orchard where trees are *already* growing is merely to let the water be better absorbed by the ground, enabling the ground to better nourish the existing growth.[25] Such ploughing is beneficial even after Pesach, despite the fact that most of the moisture has already gone out of the ground. Failure to meet the aforementioned requirements means that the trees are not considered as standing in an orchard and therefore the area around them is considered as being like a grain field,[26] ploughing being forbidden from Pesach onwards. Only an area around each tree of a distance of האורה וסלו חוצה לו (the space taken up by a fig harvester and his fig basket,[28] which is two אמות)[27(29)] may be ploughed, as this is clearly seen to be for benefit in the sixth year, since the tree is obviously now benefitting from the ploughing and no confusion will occur. If there are however, at least ten trees within an area of a *Bais Se'oh* then even if they would not produce the aforementioned amount of figs, one may plant the whole area until Shavuos[28] because[29] we see in many places[30] that ten trees are considered as being an orchard, thus whatever they could produce, the whole *Bais Se'oh* is always considered as serving the trees so that there is an *orchard* of a *Bais Se'oh*.

Even in the case where the aforementioned requirements are met and it is considered an orchard it is a dispute until when after Pesach

---

(27) These conditions being present, Bais Shammai and Bais Hillel estimated that the יניקה of each tree covers the whole area of the *Bais Se'oh*, thus the whole area of ground is in service of the trees.[22h] Thus, ploughing anywhere in the area will be for the benefit of the trees and not appear like he is ploughing to prepare the soil for Shmittoh.

(28) For further details see below no. 7.

(29) See footnote no. (12) for details of אמה.

h22. עיין חזו"א שם ס"ק ד' 23. שביעית פ"א מ"ב 24 לפי ירושלמי שם ורע"ב 25. עיין בספר קב ונקי על ירושלמי שביעית פ"ב הערות אות ג' 26. ר"ש שביעית שם 27. שנות אליהו שביעית פ"א מ"ב ד"ה "פחות מכאן" 28. שביעית פ"א מ"ד 29. לפי משנה ראשונה ד"ה "עד" 30. כגון פאה פ"ג מ"א; כלאים פ"ה מ"א

one may plough in this area. Both Bais Shammai and Bais Hillel say[31] that ploughing may only continue as long as it still benefits the soil which benefits the fruit of the *sixth year* i.e. any ploughing would not appear to be preparing the soil for the Shmittoh year, and would therefore not cause any confusion to occur. Only after this time would there be this problem and then ploughing is forbidden even if done within two אמות around the tree.[32] Bais Hillel mention that the date for this is until עצרת (Shavuos). Since Bais Shammai gave no specific date, then by Bais Hillel giving the date as being Shavuos it is automatically understood to explain[33] that Bais Shammai, who are usually the more stringent opinion, say that even before Shavuos it is forbidden.[34] The Tanna of the Mishna, however, tells us that the date of Bais Shammai is not much before Shavuos, both dates in fact being not far apart from each other.[35(30)] Before the nullification of Tosefes Shviyis by Rabbon Gamliel and his Bais Din the halocha was like Bais Hillel.[36]

Although these time periods of Bais Shammai and Bais Hillel are not an extention of the Tosefes Shviyis which is midorysa, nevertheless in their instituting these periods the period of issur melocha was extended from thirty days prior to Shmittoh to the Shavuos or Pesach before Shmittoh, depending on the type of field in question.

Why was the extended period of Tosefes Shviyis of Bais Shammai and Bais Hillel only for the melocha of חורש?

The reason why they instituted this extended period only for the melocha of חורש is because[37] it is the melocha which the posuk[(31)] is

---

(30) The Yerushalmi[35a] understands that Bais Shammai are in fact the lenient view here therefore in Bais Hillel stating "until Shavous" they mean "until Shavous *and no longer*", Bais Shammai saying "*even longer*".

(31) Or the הלכה למשה מסיני.

---

31. שביעית פ"א מ"א ועיין ברע"ב. 32. ערוך השלחן העתיד סימן י"ח ס"ק ז' 33. תוי"ט שביעית שם ד"ה "וקרובין". 34. תוס' מועד קטן ג: ד"ה "עד". 35. "וקרובין דברי אלו להיות כדברי אלו" 35a. שביעית פ"א הל' א'. 36. שביעית פ"ב מ"א 37. ר"ת ראש השנה ט: "ומותר" לפי תירץ ראשון

forbidding during Tosefes Shviyis,[32] therefore already being a Torah prohibition it would befit the Rabbonon to extend the period, albeit for a different reason (from the last thirty days of the period, which is forbidden midroysa) i.e. to avoid the above mentioned confusion. This is something which could not be done on their part with regard to the other melochos (which ostensibly could also lead to the same confusion) since the Torah itself did not forbid these melochos as Tosefes Shviyis. Another suggested reason[38] is that even if the posuk is not restricting its prohibition to ploughing[33] but also forbids זורע, זומר, קוצר ובוצר during Tosefes Shviyis,[34] חורש nevertheless differs from these melochos since it can prepare the soil for future sowing such as preparing in the sixth year for Shmittoh. Thus the benefit during Shmittoh can be related back to the ploughing before Shmittoh and this leads to the aforementioned confusion, unlike where one plants a tree[35][36] before Shmittoh, for the fact that it grows during Shmittoh will not lead one to think that the planting before Shmittoh was for it to grow during Shmittoh, just as we understand that planting many years before Shmittoh is not considered as being specially planted for Shmittoh simply because it grows also during the Shmittoh year. If this were the case then planting would always be forbidden.[37]

---

(32) This answer is according to the Rishonim who understand that this posuk is not forbidding any other melochos.[37a]

(33) This is in accordance with the other Rishonim such as the Rash.[38a]

(34) See footnote (20).

(35) נוטע which is a form of זורע (see Chapter Three "Chart of Agricultural Melochos") and therefore considered as specified in the posuk (see footnote (20)). The Rambam[38b] appears to dispute this point.

(36) Tosfos uses the example of נוטע only because the Gemora is discussing this melocha, but the same is true for זורע, זומר, קוצר, בוצר.

(37) Thus even in the period of the Mikdosh when Tosefes Shviyis was midorysa, נוטע was only forbidden thirty days before Shmittoh.[38c] When Tosefes Shviyis became nullified then miderabbonon נוטע remained forbidden thirty days before Shmittoh on account of מראית העין.[38d] See below no. 4.

37a. עיין תוס' רע"ק שביעית אות ט"ו 38. לפי תירץ שני בתוס' שם 38a. תוס' רע"ק שם 38b.
שמיטה ויובל פ"א הל' ד' 38c. תוי"ט שביעית פ"ב מ"ו 38d. תוי"ט שם.

3. The Nullification of Tosefes Shviyis

Being that Tosefes Shviyis is a din midorysa, either from a posuk or a הלכה למשה מסיני, then it has to be understood how such a din could be nullified by Rabbon Gamliel and his Bais Din.

The Gemora[39] first suggests that Rabbon Gamliel and his Bais Din drew support[40] for their nullification from a *gezera shova*.

We find the term "שבת" used in the posuk of ששת ימים תעבוד וביום השביעי תשבות בחריש ובקציר וכו'[41]. In the posuk which commands us to keep Shabbos the term "שבת" is also used ששת ימים תעבוד ועשית...ויום השביעי שבת וכו'. By way of *gezera shova* they learned that just like concerning erev Shabbos it is permissible to do melocha right up until sunset[38] so also concerning erev Shviyis it is permitted to do melocha until sunset of the day preceding Rosh Hashona. The question however posed by the Gemora is—how could Rabbon Gamliel and his Bais Din come along with their own *gezera shova* and uproot an existing prohibition of the Torah if the rule is that one cannot make their own *gezera shova* but it must be a tradition from Sinai?[42][39] The Gemora answers that the reason they could nullify such a din is rather[43] because Rabbon Gamliel and his Bais Din took the view of Rabbi Yishmoel that Tosefes Shviyis is a הלכה למשה מסיני and they could therefore annul it on account of the following:

Since the הלכה למשה מסיני of Tosefes Shviyis[40] was taught to

---

(38) There is a short period of Tosefes Shabbos (approx. two minutes) however this is considered too insignificant to be mentioned.[41a] (39) Had the *gezera shova* been traditional from Sinai then it would have dictated in the very first instance that just like there is no Tosefes for Shabbos so there is no Tosefes for Shviyis, thus the posuk בחריש ובקציר תשבות would never have been understood to teach us a din of Tosefes Shviyis.
(40) Referred to as "עשר נטיעות".

---

39. מועד קטן ד. וע"ע ירושלמי שביעית פ"א הל' א'. 40. סמכו 41. שמות כ:ט-י 41a תוס' מועד קטן שם ד"ה "מה" 42. רש"י מועד קטן שם ד"ה "אתא ג"ש" "דאינהו גמירו מנפשייהו" 43. עיין תוס' מועד קטן ד. ד"ה "אלא"

Moshe Rabeinu together with the הלכה למשה מסיני of ערבה[41] and of
ניסוח המים[42] therefore Tosefes Shviyis is being compared to ערבה and
ניסוח המים in that just as they are only applicable during the period of
the Bais haMikdosh, so also the halocha of Tosefes Shviyis is only
applicable during this time.[44]

This was also the view of Bais Shammai and Bais Hillel.[45]
However after the destruction of the Second Bais haMikdosh,
before the Bais Din of Rabbon Gamliel, Bais Shammai and Bais
Hillel decreed that the halocha of Tosefes Shviyis should still
continue miderabbonon due to the problem of people coming to
make mistakes by getting confused[46] (see above), thus any future
nullification of Tosefes Shviyis would only be a question of
nullifying this decree, and Bais Shammai with Bais Hillel instituted
their decree with the condition that a Bais Din in a later generation
could nullify it if they so wished.[47] Thus Rabbon Gamliel and his
Bais Din were able to nullify this decree.

4. שלושים יום בשנה חשובין שנה—Planting trees is forbidden forty-four
days before Shmittoh

Certain halochos, such as ערלה and נטע רבעי, involve counting the
passage of a certain number of years. The fruit which a tree
produces in the first three years of its life have a halocha of ערלה[43]
being forbidden midorysa to be eaten. The fruit of the fourth year is
called נטע רבעי, and has a halocha of being kodesh, only being
permitted to be eaten (if טהור) in Yerushalayim. If the kedusha is
redeemed onto coins then it becomes ordinary fruit which can be
eaten anywhere.[44] The fruit of the fifth year is permitted

(41) The mitzvoh of "willow reeds" i.e. walking everyday of Succos once around the
Mizbei'ach on the seventh day seven times around it. (42) Pouring of water onto the
Mizbei'ach as an offering on each day of Succos.
(43) See Chapter Five.
(44) Ibid.

44. תוס' שם 45. לפי המשמעות תפארת ישראל שם וכן כתוב בהדיה בפירוש משנה ראשונה 46.
תפארת ישראל שם 47. מועד קטן ג:

immediately for ordinary consumption after the separation of Terumos and Ma'aseros.[45]

Rabbi Meir and Rabbi Elozor differ as to how these years are to be calculated.[48] According to Rabbi Meir ״יום אחד בשנה חשוב שנה״ one day can sometimes be counted as a year. When? If a tree took root even just *one day before Rosh Hashona,* the following day, it being Rosh Hashona, is considered as the beginning of the second year of the tree's life as far as ערלה and נטעי רבעי are concerned.[46] Therefore the three years ערלה period would, in this case, be a span of two years and a day. After three years and a day on Rosh Hashona, the נטע רבעי period would have also passed and the fruit produced after this would be fifth year produce and permitted for ordinary consumption.

Rabbi Elozor disagrees and says ״שלשים יום בשנה חשובין שנה״ thirty days at times can be counted as a year. The above would be true for thirty days, but not for one day. This dispute[49] stems from the different way in which they understood the following posuk in the Torah:[50]

״ויהי באחת ושש מאות שנה בראשון באחד לחודש חרבו המים״ ''And it came to pass in the six hundredth and first year (after Creation), in the first day of the first month (of this 601st year), the waters were dried up (the earth became like a sort of mud with a crust on top—רש״י) etc''. In other words it was the first day of the 601st year.[47] Rabbi Meir learns that since the Torah refers to it as the 601st year, despite that the year was only in its first day,[51] would support that when we make certain calculations based on numbers of years (for certain halochos) then one day can already be counted as a whole year.[48]

(45) Ibid.
(46) The one day before Rosh Hashona was considered its first year.
(47) This being Rosh Hashona, the first of Tishrei, 600 years had passed since Creation and it was now the day after the end of this 600 years.
(48) Meaning that *at least* one day before Rosh Hashona can be considered as a year (so that at the commencement of Rosh Hashona it already begins the count of a

48. ראש השנה י: 49. ראש השנה שם: 50. בראשית ח:יג 51. מדאכתי יום אחד הוא דעייל בשנה

Rabbi Elozor says[52] that if the posuk would have said "ויהי בשש מאות ואחת שנה וכו'" i.e. in stating the number "601st year" it would place the word "אחת" ("first") next to the word "שנה" (year) then he would agree with Rabbi Meir that the Torah is calling one day ("אחת") a year ("שנה"). However the posuk says ויהי באחת ושש מאות "שנה" so that the word "שנה" is only next to the words "שש מאות"[53] (600 years) therefore what does "אחת" mean? It means "in the *beginning* of the first year after 600 years[49] so that the posuk reads: "And it came to pass in the *beginning* of the sixth hundredth and first year in the first month, the first day of the month etc." But it is not considered as a *whole* year as it is according to Rabbi Meir.[50]

How does Rabbi Elozor learn from this posuk that thirty days can be counted as a complete year? From the end of the posuk. It says "בראשון באחד לחודש" "in the first month (of this 601st year) the first day of this month". Thus, the word "אחד" (first day) has been placed next to the word "לחודש" (month), therefore the Torah is calling one day, a month,[54(51)] and yet the Torah refers to it as having already been a whole month.[52] Now, since a month is made up of units[55] of days[53] as is seen from the posuk which says[56] "חדש ימים" "a month of days", and we see from the posuk here which says "בראשון באחד לחודש" that one unit (a day) of this period (month) can be counted as this whole period which it is a unit of, therefore it is a בנין אב[54] to tell us a rule that one unit of a period can be counted (with respect to certain Halochic calculations) as the whole period. Therefore since a year is made up of units of months[57] as is seen from the posuk which says[58] "לחדשי השנה" "months of a year" and a month is

second year,) certainly any more than one day before Rosh Hashona can be counted as a year.

(49) i.e. In the beginning of the sixth hundredth and first year.
(50) Rabbi Meir learns that "אחת" can nevertheless be related to "שנה".
(51) i.e. The first month of the 601st year.
(52) i.e. It is referred to as "the first month."
(53) Termed חודש נמנה בימים.
(54) See Chapter Three no.1 footnote (1).

52. ואידך 53. שנה אשש מאות קאי 54. מדאכתי יום אחד הוא דעייל בחודש 55. מנויין 56. במדבר
יא:כ 57. שנה נמנה בחדשיים 58. שמות יב:ב

usually 30 days, therefore 30 days can be counted as one whole year.[55]

We pasken according to Rabbi Elozor,[59] and this leads to the following problem:[60] If one plants a fruit tree so that it takes root *within* 30 days of Rosh Hashona of the Shmittoh year e.g. 29 days or less before Rosh Hashona, then when Rosh Hashona commences it is only the beginning of the count of its *first* year and the 29 days previous to Rosh Hashona do not count at all. Therefore when people see that he begins eating the fruit of this tree only after the commencement of the Rosh Hashona which completes three years and begins its fourth year after Rosh Hashona of the Shmittoh year, they will think he planted it during Shmittoh. The planting, therefore, constitutes an act which involves מראית העין, which is an act which can arouse unwarranted suspicion that a transgression is being committed. In order to prevent such מראית העין the Rabbonon decreed that one may only plant a fruit tree before Rosh Hashona of the Shmittoh year if it will take root *before* 30 days to its commencement so that on Rosh Hashona of the Shmittoh year it already begins the count of its second year, and he can begin eating its fruit already on the Rosh Hashona which ends only two years after Rosh Hashona of the Shmittoh year. Thus it will clearly prove to the onlooker that he must have planted well before the Shmittoh year.

We pasken[61] like Rabbi Yossi and Rabbi Shimon[62] that it takes 14 days[63] for a tree to take root. Thus, only after 14 days can the tree be considered as having been *planted.*

---

(55) Meaning that *at least* thirty days before Rosh Hashona can be counted as a year and certainly any more than thirty days before Rosh Hashona can be counted as a year, See footnote(48).

---

59. רמב״ם הל׳ נטע רבעי פ״ט הל׳ ח׳ ושו״ע יו״ד סימן רצ״ד סעיף ד׳ 60. עי׳ חזו״א שביעית סי׳ י״ז ס״ק כ״ג 61. רמב״ם שמיטה ויובל פ״ג הל׳ י״א ועי׳ חזו״א שביעית סימן כ״ב ס״ק ה׳ 62. שביעית פ״ב מ״ו 63. לשתי שבתות

Therefore the halocha[64] is that one may only plant a fruit tree up until 44 days before Rosh Hashona of the Shmittoh year.

—

5. Other melochos prohibited forty-four days before Shmittoh

Any melocha which can lead to the above mentioned מראית העין is forbidden to be done 44 days before Shmittoh. It is, therefore, forbidden to layer vines[65] 44 days before Shmittoh if one cuts the branch which was inserted into the ground so that it is no longer connected to the vine it came from[66(56)] and its source of nourishment now comes directly from the ground. Thus it is like a newly planted tree, the fruit it now bears in the next three years have a din of ערלה, therefore involving the problem of מראית העין.

It is also forbidden to graft (הרכבה) the branch of one tree onto another tree within 44 days[67] of the Shmittoh year; for the following reason:

There is a halocha that if one plants fruit trees with the intention for them to serve merely as a fence[68] around a certain area of land, then even though these trees produce fruit they have no din of ערלה[69] and the fruits are permitted to be eaten even within the first three year after its plantation.(57) Thus if one planted a fruit tree, to act as a fence, within 44 days of the Shmittoh year there would be no problem of מראית העין since there would be no counting of years for Orlah. However, if one then (within 44 days of Shmittoh) grafted onto this tree a branch with the intention that the fruit that this particular branch bears should be for eating purposes then there would have to begin a count of years for Orlah on this fruit and there would be the problem of מראית העין.[70] If one had planted the fruit tree

---

(56) This is referred to as being פסקה מן האב.

(57) Unless one changed their mind within these three years and decided to use the fruits primarily for eating.[69a]

---

64. רמב"ם שם 65. רמב"ם שם 66. עיין חזו"א שביעית סימן כ"ב ס"ק ה' ד"ה "במש"כ" ועי' בספר המצוות התלויות בארץ סי' כ"ו ס"ק ו' 67. רמב"ם שם 68. היינו לסייג 69. ערלה פ"א מ"א 69a. תוס' רע"ק ערלה אות א' 70. עי' חזו"א שביעית סימן כ"ב ס"ק ה' וסימן כ"ה ס"ק י"ג

many years before the Shmittoh year then some authorities[71] are of the view that it would be permitted to graft a branch onto the tree with the purpose of eating its fruit, even within 44 days of the Shmittoh year, because true it is now bearing fruit for eating purposes and this fruit is therefore suitable to have a count of years for Orlah, nevertheless the tree itself remains with its status as acting as a fence and therefore the counting of the years for the Orlah of this fruit is reckoned from when the actual tree was planted. In the case where it was planted more than three years before the Shmittoh year then there would be no מראית העין with grafting since the count of Orlah would have already passed.

The Chazon Ish[72] writes that had it not been for these authorities then he would have suggested that even if the tree was planted many years before the Shmittoh year it would be forbidden to graft a branch onto it within 44 days of the Shmittoh year for the purpose of producing fruit to eat, because the very *act* of this grafting should change the status of the tree making it now considered producing fruits primarily for eating and therefore the count of years for Orlah should start from this very moment of time.

Concerning the sowing of grains, legumes, vegetables and flowers then there is no problem of מראית העין since they have no din of Orlah. The Chazon Ish,[73] however, first suggests that maybe it is forbidden to sow them close to the Shmittoh year if they will strike root (קליטה) during the Shmittoh year. This is because the Torah concerning Shmittoh speaks of "שביתת הארץ" i.e. that the land should rest, thereby including that it should not be sown.[(58)] However the Chazon Ish concludes[74] that since such a thing is not mentioned anywhere in the Gemora or in the poskim therefore this does not apply.

(58) Striking root is the act of sowing.[73a]

71. הרמב"ן והגר"א הובא בחזו"א שם 72. שביעית שם ד"ה "מיהו' 73. שביעית סימן י"ז ס"ק כ"ה
73a. חזו"א שם קליטה הוא זריעה ממש 74. שביעית סימן כ"ב ס"ק ה' ד"ה "במש"כ"

6. What constitutes an orchard (שדה אילן)?

It is explained[75] that permission to plough a whole *Bais Se'oh* with three trees until Shavous for the benefit of the trees is only as long as the distance between each tree is no more than 33.3 אמה[59]. The reason why the whole area of the *Bais Se'oh* may be ploughed is only on account of the fact that the trees draw their sustenance from every part of this area, and therefore it can be considered an area belonging to (i.e. in service of) the trees. That is, the Gemora[76] brings that the "יניקה" ("Yenikah", i.e., the area of ground from which the tree draws its sustenance)[60] of a tree covers a distance of 16.66 אמה radiating from all sides of the tree. This means that each tree has its own circular area of land having a radius of 16.66 אמה from which it draws its sustenance. Consequently, the area of sustenance for three trees is a *Bais Se'oh* (i.e., being that the radius from which each tree draws its sustenance is 16.66 אמה, and the area of a circle with a radius of 16.66 אמה is 833.3 אמה[i.e.,this is using the correct figure of Pi which is "3" being that this is the number which the Gemora works with[77]]. Therefore the total area of the יניקה of three trees when they are positioned in a way that the יניקה of the trees do not overlap [i.e. when there is a distance of 33.3 אמה between the trees,]

(59) For the measurement of an אמה. See footnote (12)

(60) The roots of a tree can extend for 25 אמה, however only 16.6 אמה of root which is closest to the tree draws sustenance.[76a]

75. על פי חזו"א שביעית סי' י"ז ס"ק ד' על פי בבא בתרא כו:-כז. 76. בבא בתרא שם 76a. רש"י בבא בתרא כו: ד"ה "בתוך שש עשרה אמה" 77. עיין חזו"א או"ח סימן קל"ח ס"ק ד'

is three times this amount of area, 2500 אמה which is described in square אמות giving the figure of 50 אמה by 50 אמה, which is a *Bais Se'oh*). Therefore one can either have the shape of the *Bais Se'oh* like this:

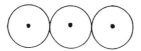

or like this [78]

and it is questionable if one is only permitted to plough in a circle around each tree, i.e.

or if one can plough in straight lines, thereby ploughing a larger area[79] i.e.

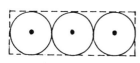

78. חזו"א שביעית סימן י"ז ס"ק ד' ד"ה "שביעית" 79 חזו"א שם ד"ה "לעולם"

If there is a distance of more than 33.3 אמה between two of the trees, then it is not a case of three trees within an area of a *Bais Se'oh* and each tree is considered separately in which case it is not an orchard and one may not plough the whole *Bais Se'oh* from Pesach until Shavuos. One may only plough from Pesach until Shavuos around each tree a radius being the amount of distance required by the fig harvester and his basket into which he puts his figs (to be explained), i.e. 2 אמות,[80] and the rest of the field is considered like a grain field, which can only be ploughed until Pesach.[81] It is further explained[82] that if there are more than three trees, e.g. four trees, then in order for four trees to require an area of *Bais Se'oh* for their יניקה, there can be less distance than 33.3 אמה between each tree, and so the more trees there are, the less distance there needs to be between them in order to be able to plough the whole *Bais Se'oh*, as long as there is no less than four אמות between each tree[(61)]. However, if they are positioned not closer than four אמות but are so close together that between them they would not draw their sustenance from a whole *Bais Se'oh*, then they would not receive a din of an orchard and one would only be permitted until Shavuos to plough two אמות around them.[(62)] It is further explained[83] that as far as the ground which lies

(61) Less than four אמות between trees is an unusual positioning and means that they are awaiting removal[82a] therefore the area is considered like a grain field[82b,] already from Pesach one may not plough there at all.

(62) However according to other Achronim[82c] even if the trees are closer together (not closer than four אמות) one may plough the whole *Bais Se'oh*. The reason being because this speaks of older trees which are big and have long branches, therefore even if they are close together the whole *Bais Se'oh* can be seen to have a connection to them.[82d]

80. שנות אליהו ד"ה "פחות מכאן" 81. שביעית פ"ב מ"א 82. חזו"א שם 82a. ערוך השלחן העתיד סימן י"ח ס"ק ז' 82b. פירוש הרא"ש 82c. תפא"י אות ה' ופני משה פ"א הל' ה' ד' ד"ה "הכא כולן נתונין במקום אחד" 82d. פני משה שם וערוך השלחן העתיד סימן י"ח ס"ק י"ט. 83. חזו"א שביעית סי' י"ז ס"ק ד' ד"ה "לעולם"

between the trees is concerned, then the whole area of it may be ploughed, i.e.

but as far as the part of the ground which lies beyond the trees is concerned, then one may only plough an area which is half the distance between the trees, i.e., in the case of three trees where the distance between each tree is 33.3 אמה then one may plough up until 16.6 אמה going from the outside of each tree, i.e..

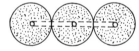

It is interesting to note that the Yerushalmi[84] interprets the Mishna differently than the Bavli. According to the Yerushalmi the יניקה only extends for 8 אמה (as opposed to 16.6 אמה for the Bavli) and the trees must be so positioned (in order to be able to plough the entire *Bais Se'oh*) that a square of a *Bais Se'oh* is thereby made, i.e., each tree occupying an area of .6 אמה. The distance between each tree is 16

84. שביעית פרק א׳ הל׳ ב׳ מתוך התמיה של רבי אלעזר ״מזו לזו שש עשרה ולצד עשרים וחמש!? עי׳ ברש״ס שרבי אלעזר שאל כאן על הפשט של הגמרא לגבי המשנה כל שלשה אילנות לבית סאה מגמ׳ בלא יחפור

אמה so that their יניקה is not overlapping and the two outer sides of the trees until the border is a distance of 8 אמה on each side.

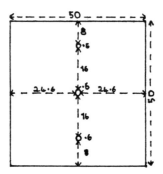

This therefore excludes a case of where there would only be for example 15 אמה distance between the trees, since this would not add up to an entire area of a *Bais Se'oh*.

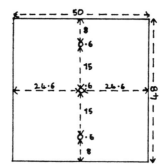

The Tiferes Yisroel[85] learns that the positioning of the trees is immaterial, as long as they are at least four אמות apart, then a square, the area of a *Bais Se'oh*, is drawn around them, the trees being in the center and this entire area may be ploughed.

The Yerushalmi[86] points out that the Mishna here speaks of an
open area of a *Bais Se'oh*, and questions as to how the trees could be
positioned if there was a fence on one border of the *Bais Se'oh*.
Perhaps, now that the *Bais Se'oh* is clearly delineated on one side,
even if the trees were not dispersed throughout the *Bais Se'oh* but
three trees were standing next to the fence one could still plough the
entire *Bais Se'oh* i.e.,

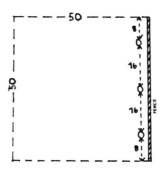

and that if this would be the halocha then in the case of where there
is a fence on all sides of an area, one should be able to have three
trees in an area of בית ארבעת סאין, i.e., an area a size of four *Bais
Se'oh* and plough all of it until Shavuos, i.e.,

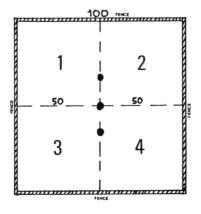

86. שביעית פ״א הל׳ ב׳ ״רבי שמואל בר רב יצחק בעי״

in which case it would mean that when the Mishna here speaks of being חורש a '*Bais Se'oh*' it only refers to three trees standing in an open area.

7. מלא האורה וסלו חוצה לו

In a case where a tree is not considered part of an orchard (see above no. 6) then already from Pesach before Shmittoh one may only plough an amount of land around the tree a distance of מלא האורה וסלו חוצה לו[86a]

The term מלא האורה וסלו means the amount of distance taken up by the fig harvester and the basket into which he puts the figs. "חוצה לו" can be interpreted in two ways. 1) That this distance is measured from the end of the branches going outwards[87] (the words "חוצה לו" mean "outside of *the tree*"). In other words, one may plough all the soil which is directly under the branches plus a distance of "האורה וסלו", going out from the end of the branches.[88] The harvester takes up a distance of one אמה, and his basket takes up a distance of one אמה,[89] therefore one may plough going outwards from the end of the branches a radius of two אמות around the tree, since this amount of area in being required for the harvester and his basket is thereby in service of the tree.[90] 2) The Tiferes Yisroel learns that the word "לו" refers to the harvester and therefore the words מלא

86a. שביעית פ״א מ״ב 87. רש״ס, ועי׳ בחזו״א שביעית סימן י״ז ס״ק ט״ו ורע״ב לפי תוס׳ אנשי שם
88. חזו״א שם 89. שנות אליהו ד״ה ״פחות מכאן״ 90. לפי משנת יוסף עמוד נ׳ באמצע ס״ק ח׳

האורה וסלו חוצה לו״ mean "the amount of distance *required* by the fig harvester and his basket into which he puts the figs when the basket is placed on the outside of him. That is, when the basket is placed on the outside of him then a longer distance is taken up by him and his basket, than when the basket is placed between himself and the tree.

This distance is measured from the tree trunk and here is a smaller area than according to the first opinion. The rest of the field is considered as a grain field, which can only be ploughed until Pesach.

CHAPTER FIVE

DETERMINING TO WHICH YEAR A CROP BELONGS

1. The need to know which year a crop belongs

There are several instances where there is a need to clarify which year a particular crop belongs:-

Terumos and Ma'aseros

There is a seven year cycle[1] concerning the separation of Terumos and Ma'aseros from grain,[2] grape wine and olive oil grown in Eretz Yisroel.[1] That is, during the first six years of this cycle the Torah commands us to separate from grain, grape wine and olive oil[2] the following:[3]

a) תרומה גדולה

The Torah[3] commands us to remove even the tiniest amount and give it to a Kohen.

b) מעשר ראשון

The Torah[4] commands us that after we have separated Terumah Gedolah we must then remove one tenth from the remainder of the crop and give it to a Levi.

c) תרומת מעשר   The Torah[5] commands the Levi to separate one tenth of the Ma'aser Rishon which he was given, and give it to a Kohen.

---

(1) This is learned from the Torah by way of a Kabbola of the Rabbonon.[1a]

(2) This refers to the חמשת מינים[1b] being wheat, barley, spelt, rye, oat[1c].

(3) The following is a brief introduction to the main subject, which is the title of this chapter.

1a. מתוך דברי רמב"ן דברים יד: כב וז"ל וטעם שנה שיעשר אותו שני שנים זו אחר זו כפי קבלת רבותינו וכו' 1b. רמב"ן שם וז"ל ופירוש דגן בלשון הקודש "חמשת המינים הידועין בתבואה" 1c. עיין מ"ב סימן ר"ח ס"ק ב 1. קידושין לז. ורמב"ם הל' תרומות פ"א הל' א' 2. רמב"ן שם ד"ה "וטעם שנה שנה וכו' 3. דברים יח: ד 4. במדבר יח: כד 5. במדבר יח: כו

d) מעשר שני

The Torah[6] commands that we separate another tenth and take it to Yerushalayim and eat it there, or if it is too difficult to bring this tenth to Yerushalayim, then its kedusha may be transferred onto their equivalent value of coins, and this money is brought to Yerushalayim and spent on food, especially cattle to be used for קרבן שלמים the flesh of which is eaten either by the owner of the original crop, or by any other Jew, with a portion going to the Kohen.

However, during the third and sixth year of the seven year cycle the Torah[7] commands us that instead of separating a tenth as מעשר שני we must separate it as מעשר עני i.e. it must be given to the poor

Consequently we see the need to know if produce is third or sixth year crop in order to know whether the separation of the last tenth is to be מעשר עני instead of מעשר שני.[8] In addition,[9] since the Torah [10] tells us that one may not separate Terumos and Ma'aseros from produce of one year for produce of another year,(4) it is necessary to know to which year a crop is considered belonging.

Shmittoh

הפקר

During the seventh year (Shmittoh) the Torah[11] commands us that we must let the land rest and everyone must have an equal right to any produce growing in Eretz Yisroel i.e. the produce is to be הפקר, (ownerless).(5) There is no obligation to separate Terumos and Ma'aseros from הפקר produce.[12]

(4) מעשר or תרומה need not be separated from the food needed for present consumption, other, as yet untithed produce can be used

(5) It is a dispute amongst the Achronim whether one is obligated to make an actual declaration that his produce is free for public [11a] use (ownerless), or whether the

6. דברים יד: כב 7. דברים כו: יב עי' ברש"י ד"ה "שנת המעשר" 8. רע"ב ראש השנה פ"א מ"א ד"ה "ראש השנה לאילן" 9. רע"ב שם 10. דברים יד: כד ועי' תרומות פ"א מ"ה 11. שמות כג: י-יא ויקרא כה: ה: א'-ז' 11a. בית יוסף , אבקת רוכל

קדושת שביעית

Shmittoh produce has *Kedushas Shviyis*. The Torah[13] says"כי" "יובל היא קודש תהיה לכם מן השדה תאכלו את תבואתה" "for it is the Yovel, it shall be holy to you, you shall eat its produce from the field." The Gemora[14] learns[15] from the seeming redundancy of the word "היא" that just as the ground during Yovel has kedusha in that one may not work it, so also its produce has kedusha, therefore one must treat it so by only eating it and not causing its הפסד (waste).(6)(7) Shmittoh produce also has this halocha being that concerning the land and its produce Shmittoh and Yovel have one and the same din.[16]

שביעית תופסת דמיה

A Beraisa[17] teaches us that money given in exchange for Shmittoh produce takes on the same kedusha as the produce (שביעית תופסת דמיה). This being derived also from the above mentioned posuk which says"קודש תהיה לכם", in speaking here of קודש it tells us that its din is similar to that of *Hekdesh* (property of the Bais haMikdosh). Just like money given in exchange for *Hekdesh* "grasps" kedusha from it,(8) so also money given in exchange for Yovel and Shmittoh

---

produce automatically becomes ownerless at the commencement of Shmittoh[11b] (termed "שביעית אפקעתא דמלכא היא". The Chazon Ish[11c] paskens like the latter.

(6) Others[15a] understand the drosha differently i.e because the end of the posuk says "תאכלו את תבואתה" therefore there is a *hekesh* between יובל and תבואה, just like יובל has kedusha so does its produce, only when it is called "תבואה" does it have kedusha. This is when it reaches the stage of עונת המעשרות, see footnote (17).

(7) It is on account of this that the Torah earlier[15b] tells us that Shmittoh produce is "לאכלה" "to eat it" and not to do business with it or waste it.[15c]

(8) Derived from "פדה בערכך"[17a]

11b. מבי"ט סימן מ"ב11c. שביעית סימן י' ס"ק ה' ד"ה "ואע"ג" סימן י"ט ס"ק כ"ד 12. רש"י ראש השנה טו. ד"ה "יד כל ממשמשים בה" 13. ויקרא כה: יב 14. ירושלמי שביעית פ"ד הל' ז' 15 לפי פני משה שם 15a. מהר"א פולדא על ירושלמי שם 15b. ויקרא כה: ו 15c. תורה תמימה 16. רש"י סוכה מ: ד"ה "בשנת היובל" 17. סוכה שם 17a. ויקרא כז: כז עיין רש"י עבודה זרה נ: ד"ה "קדש תופס את דמיו"

produce "grasps" kedusha. However unlike *Hekdesh,* Shmittoh produce does not lose its kedusha in the exchange since the Torah here says "קודש תהיה" "holy shall it be", it shall always be in its original holy status.[18]

Consequently we see the need to know if produce is seventh year crop in order to know if it is exempt from the separation of Terumos and Ma'aseros, and if it is to be treated as *Kedushas Shviyis.*

Orlah

The Torah[19] tells us that for the first three years after the planting [9] of a fruit tree, the fruits which it bears are Orlah (ערלה.) That is, they are closed up and barred,[20] meaning that we may not derive any benefit from the fruit. However, the fruit which the tree bears during the fourth year, termed "נטע רבעי", is kodesh and has dinim similar to מעשר שני i.e. the fruit must be eaten in Yerushalayim or their kedusha redeemed with money.[10] The fruit of the fifth year and onwards after plantation is considered as regular fruit without any restrictions on it.

We therefore see that it is neccessary to know if the fruits of a tree are from the third or fourth year after plantation, or if they are from the fifth year or more after plantation.

2. The factors which determine to which year fruit and other produce belongs

(9) The time when the tree strikes its roots in the ground, fourteen days after the initial planting in the soil, see chapter four.

(10) There is no obligation to separate Terumos and Ma'aseros from נטע רבעי. [20a]

---

18. בהוויתה תהא 19. ויקרא יט: כג 20. רש״י על הפסוק שם 20a. ירושלמי פאה פ״ז סוף הל׳ ה׳ ומעשר שני פ״ה סוף הל׳ ב׳ ועיין רמב״ם מעשר שני פ״ט הל׳ ד׳

חנטה

The Mishna[21] informs us that the beginning of a new year concerning the plantation of a fruit tree is from the first day of Tishrei (Rosh Hashona). The Gemora[22] explains that we derive this from the following:

The Torah [23] says "ובחודש השביעי באחד לחודש מקרא קדש יהיה לכם...יום תרועה יהיה לכם" ''The first day of the seventh month (i.e. 1st of Tishrei)...shall be a holy day *(Yom Tov)* to you...a day to you of blowing the horn (shofar).'' Nowhere in this posuk does it state that it is a *Yom Din* (day of judgement). From where do we know that the 1st of Tishrei is a day of judgement?

The Gemora derives this from two p'sukim in Tehillim.[24] "תקעו בחודש שופר, בכסה ליום חגנו" ''blow shofar at the time of the new moon on the Chag (Yom Tov) when the moon is covered (i.e. hidden from our sight)''. Which *Yom Tov* do we have when it is a day that the moon is covered, i.e. a new moon? It is Rosh Hashona, the 1st of Tishrei.

The next posuk goes on to state "כי חק לישראל הוא משפט לאלקי יעקב" ''for it is an ordinance to Yisroel, it is a day of judgement for the G-d of Ya'akov''.

We know from the above that the 1st of Tishrei is the day on which we are judged. The Torah says elsewhere[25] "מרשית השנה ועד אחרית השנה" ''from the beginning of the year until the end of the year'' and the Gemora explains this posuk to mean that at the beginning of the year there is a judgement in that it is decided by HaShem what will be up to the end of it, therefore "מרשית השנה" refers to the 1st of Tishrei.

By way of *gezera shova* of the word "שנה" in the posuk here "מרשית *השנה*" and the word "שנה" in the posuk concerning Orlah "שלש שנים" we learn that just as "מרשית השנה" יהיה לכם ערלים *ובשנה הרביעית*"

21. ראש השנה פ״א מ״א 22. ראש השנה ח. -ח: 23. במדבר כט: א' 24. תהלים פא: ד' וה' 25. דברים יא: יב

refers to the 1st of Tishrei so also "ובשנה הרביעית" refers to the year of planting as beginning the 1st of Tishrei.

Accordingly, if a fruit tree takes root at least 30 days before the 1st of Tishrei then the 1st of Tishrei will mark the beginning of its second year.[11]

It was mentioned in the previous chapter that it normally takes 14 days for a tree to strike root, and therefore if one plants a fruit tree 44 days before Rosh HaShona then Rosh Hashona marks the beginning of its second year. The following Rosh HaShona marks the beginning of its third year and the following Rosh HaShona marks the beginning of the count of its fourth year after plantation. However, the fruit has a din of נטע רביעי only *after* the 15th of Sh'vat of its fourth year. Any fruit it bears before the 15th of Sh'vat is still considered third year produce and has a din of Orlah. This is because as far as the fruit is concerned, their new year begins on the 15th of Sh'vat.[26] In other words, there are two orders of counting:
1) The number of years considered to have passed since the tree's planting, each Rosh Hashona (1st of Tishrei) marking the beginning of a new year.

2) What year the fruit is considered as belonging to. Each year begins on the 15th of Sh'vat.

The reason why there are two orders of calculation for counting the years of a fruit tree is explained in the Gemora.[27] The posuk[28] concerning Orlah speaks of the fruit being Orlah for the first three years, "שלש שנים יהיה לכם ערלים לא יאכל". It immediately states in the next posuk "ובשנה הרביעית יהיה כל פריו קודש" "and in the fourth year etc". The rule of ו"ו מוסיף על ענין ראשון[12] is applied[29] and therefore

(11) See Chapter Four for the subject of 30 days before Rosh Hashona being considered a whole year.

(12) The word "ו" ("and") comes to say that what is to follow maybe added, i.e. applies to what was previously stated.

26. ראש השנה פ"א מ"א לפי בית הלל 27. ראש השנה י. 28. ויקרא יט: כג 29. רש"י בגמ' שם

we can read here: "the fruit is Orlah for three years *and* in the fourth year". How are we to understand this?

It is explained[30] that the Torah here refers to a case of where although the tree has passed the Rosh Hashona which brought it into its fourth year, its fruits reached the חנטה stage of development[13] *before* the 15th of Sh'vat, and on account of this they are considered as belonging to the third year produce which have a din of Orlah. If they would have reached the חנטה stage of development *after* the 15th of Sh'vat then they would have a din of fourth year produce and not be forbidden as Orlah.

Thus, had it not been for the posuk of ובשנה הרביעית, one might have assumed that the new year of the plantation of a tree (1st of Tishrei) is the only Rosh Hashona which is applicable to a tree, and the din of Orlah of the fruits is dependent on how many years after the plantation of the tree it is. The Torah now points out that even *after* the Rosh Hashona which begins the fourth year, its fruits still have a din of third year fruit, and therefore we see that there must be *another* Rosh Hashona involved here which concerns its fruit and is after the 1st of Tishrei. We therefore have to find a set date[31] as to when this other Rosh Hashona is. It is the 15th of Sh'vat because on this date the fruit of a tree goes into the stage of חנטה.[14] The Chazal came to this date by the fact that this is the only stage of the growth of the fruit which has a set date to occur on since this stage of development occurs immediately after most of the winter rains have fallen.[32] Although the stage of development referred to as הבאת

---

(13)   When the formation of the fruit appears blossoming out. See "Shmittoh in General" no. 1 for details and diagrams.

(14)   Therefore concerning the fruit of a tree their years are counted from the 15th of Sh'vat to the 15th of the following Sh'vat. *13a Concerning all other species their years are counted from the 1st of Tishrei to the 1st of the following Tishrei31b and although the Mishna only mentions vegetables* (ירקות) *it means to include grains as well.31c*

---

30. רש״י בגמ׳ שם ור״ש שביעית פ״ב מ״ז 31. יום קבוע 31a. ראש השנה פ״א מ״א לפי בית הלל 31b. ראש השנה שם "באחד בתשרי ר״ה...ולירקות" 31c. עיין תוס׳ רע״ק שם אות ד׳ 32. ר״ש שביעית שם ועי׳ ראש השנה יד.

שליש [15] occurs after the stage of חנטה and therefore is also after the 1st of Tishrei, nevertheless it has no set date on which it occurs,[33] and the same is for any of the other stages of the development of a fruit (see below).

It is further explained[34] that even though the above mentioned drosha concerns the posuk which speaks of Orlah, nevertheless the intention of the Torah here is not to teach us a specific din concerning 'Orlah' but is rather coming to teach us a din as to what stage of development of a fruit of a tree determines the fruit as produce of that year,[16] i.e. that as far as their fruit is concerned what determines them as belonging to produce of a particular year is if their stage of חנטה, which is normally on the 15th of Sh'vat, takes place in that year.

Therefore all fruit which have their חנטה during the Shmittoh year are considered as Shmittoh produce [35][17] (fruit of the seventh year) and have *Kedushas Shviyis*.[18] Fruit which had their חנטה in the sixth year and still happen to be growing on the tree after Rosh Hashona

(15) See "Shmittoh in General" no. 2 and below.

(16) The Rash[34a] brings a proof for this from the fact that the Gemora[34b] derives that what determines grain as belonging to produce of a particular year so that we know from which year produce to separate *Ma'aseros* on it, is if it reaches the first third of its growth (הבאת שליש) within this year, and this is derived from a posuk concerning *Shmittoh* (see below). Therefore rather than teaching us a specific din of Shmittoh, the posuk teaches us a din as to what stage of development of grain determines it as produce of that year.

(17) One will notice that the Rambam[35a] says that it is reaching the stage of עונת המעשרות (according to the Rambam[35b] this is the time it becomes an edible fruit. The implication, however, of the Rambam elsewhere[35c] is not like this, which remains a difficulty.[35d]) during the Shmittoh year which determines tree fruit to be considered Shmittoh produce. This is in fact the stage of חנטה.[35e]

(18) If the 15th of Sh'vat, being the time of its חנטה, occurs during Shmittoh then this tells us that it is Shmittoh produce, however this also tells us that all the halochos of Shmittoh will apply to the tree from the 1st of Tishrei of Shmittoh.[35f]

33. ר"ש שם 34. ר"ש שם 34a. שם 34b. ראש השנה יג: 35. רמב"ם שמיטה ויובל פ"ד הל' ט' ועיין בהר"י קורקוס 35a. שם 35b. פיה"מ מעשרות פ"א מ"ב ורע"ב שם 35c. הלכות מעשר פ"ב הל' ה' 35d. עיין משנה ראשונה שם 35e. הר"י קורקוס 35f. תוס' רע"ק ראש השנה אות ה'

of the Shmittoh year are produce of the sixth year and have no
Kedushas Shviyis.[36]

הבאת שליש

The Gemora[37] tells us that as far as תבואה וזיתים (grain, grapes[19]
and olives) are concerned then what determines them as belonging
to produce of a particular year is if they complete the first third of
their ripeness (הבאת שליש) within this year.[20] Some legumes also
have this din.[38] This is derived from the fact that the Torah[39]
concerning the Shmittoh year states: "ועשת את התבואה לשלש השנים"
i.e. HaShem tells us that He will give us a bounty in the sixth year so
that "it shall make (bring forth) תבואה for three years". The Gemora
brings a drosha—do not read "לשׁלשׁ" but read "לשלש" i.e. "the תבואה
becomes made (is considered as "תבואה") when it is a third ripe".[40]

לקיטה

The Gemora[41] informs us that as far as ירקות (vegetables) are
concerned then what determines them as belonging to produce of a
particular year is if they have their לקיטה (picking) within this year.
Rabbi Yossi haG'llily and Rabbi Akiva are in dispute as to how we
arrive at this fact.

Rabbi Yossi haG'llily

Any crop ready to be picked is also mature (ripe) and can be
called "produce". It would seem that the time of picking would be
the logical determining point as to which year a crop belongs. Rabbi

---

(19) The word "תבואה" includes grain and grapes.[37a]
(20) "This year" meaning from the 1st of Tishrei to the 1st of the following Tishrei,
because as mentioned in footnote (14) the only produce which has its own Rosh
Hashona is tree fruit. Although the Rambam[37b] says that it is reaching the stage of
עונת המעשרות (see footnote (17)) during the Shmittoh year which determines תבואה
and קטניות to be considered Shmittoh produce, this is in fact the stage of הבאת שליש.[37c]

---

36. רמב״ם שמיטה ויובל שם 37. ראש השנה יג: 37a. רש״י ראש השנה יב: ד״ה ״התבואה״ 37b.
שם 37c. הר״י קורקוס 38. תוספתא שביעית פ״ב אות י׳ ועיין רמב״ם שמיטה ויובל פ״ד הל׳ י׳
ורדב״ז שם. 39. ויקרא כה: כא 40. לפי רש״י ותוס׳ שם 41. ראש השנה יד.

Yossi HaG'lilly, however, shows from p'sukim that there is another factor which determines to which year a crop belongs.

The Torah says that what determines wheat, grapes and olives as belonging to produce of a particular year is if they grow a third of their ripeness within this year (see above under "הבאת שליש"). Thus the Torah here informs us that as far as these species are concerned then what is called "maturity" (to be called "produce")[21] is not when it is ready to be picked, but at the point it reaches a third of its full future maturity. For them to grow to this third they continually need water, the later growth being nourished from this water. This means that what the Torah considers to be the dertermining factor as to which year these particular produce will belong is not dependent on readiness for picking but is rather dependent on which year they draw their primary life source (water).[42][22]

Thus if wheat grows its first third before the 1st of Tishrei then its life source was from the year preceding the 1st of Tishrei. When its fully ripe and picked after the 1st of Tishrei, if other wheat is being used to ma'aser it then this other wheat must also be produce which reached a third of its maturity before the first of Tishrei, i.e the preceding year.[43][23]

The Torah [44] states: "חג הסוכות תעשה לך שבעת ימים באספך מגרנך ומיקבך" "Chag haSuccos you shall make at the time when you gather in the produce of your threshing floor (wheat) and your wine and olive[24] press". The Chazal use this posuk as an *Asmachta* in their

---

(21) Thereby being considered *produce of this year* i.e. when it can be called "produce" it becomes produce of this year.

(22) i.e. the שליש grew from these waters ("שליש שלהן היא גדילתו"). This water can be considered as having caused its *growth* because a third ripe can be considered as the produce having *grown* since it could even be reaped at this stage under extenuating circumstances ("שמאותה שעה ראויה ליקצר בדוחק").

(23) So that there is no problem of תורמין מן החדש על הישן see footnote (4).

(24) "יקב" includes grapes and olives.[44a]

42. "שהלכה בהן אחר שנה שגדלו במימיה" 43. "ומתעשרין לשנה שעברה" גמ' 44. דברים טז:יג

44a. רש"י במדבר יח: כז ד"ה "וכמלאה מן היקב"

determination of the time when the obligation of separating Ma'aser from vegetables is to commence.[25] That is,[45] being that the Torah here speaks of 'gathering' together with 'wheat, grapes and olives', then we make a drosha that the Torah here is telling us that any produce which you gather should be similar in halacha to that of wheat, grapes and olives, that what determines them as belonging to a particular year is the year from which it draws its primary life source (the water it requires to grow by). Concerning fruit trees, the sap which causes the fruit to grow, only rises after it has taken the water it requires and this occurs just before the חנטה of the fruit.[46][26] Therefore what determines the particular year for tree fruit is the year in which it has its חנטה[27]

Concerning vegetables (ירקות), they are constantly growing from water right up until the time they are picked[47] (לקיטה), therefore if they are picked after the 1st of Tishrei then being that their life source was still from this year then it is considered as produce of this year. Consequently if the Ma'aser separated for it is from other vegetables these other vegetables must also be produce of this year.[48][28]

Rabbi Akiva

Rabbi Akiva learns that the determination of produce being considered produce of a particular year always remains dependent on maturity, and when the Torah tells us that what determines wheat, grapes or olives as belonging to produce of a particular year is if they complete the first third of their ripeness within this year---then this informs us that as far as these species are concerned then what is called "maturity" (to be called "produce")[29] is earlier

(25) Such an obligation is miderabbonon.[44b]
(26) i.e. The sap rises up the tree by means of nourishment from water, after this there is no more need for water, and the fruit develops by nourishing from the sap.
(27) Because this has been the year from which it drew its required water.
(28) See footnote (23)
(29) See footnote (21)

44b. רמב״ם תרומות פ״ב הל׳ ו׳ 45. לפי רש״י ראש השנה שם ד״ה ״באספך בגרנך ומיקבך״
46. רש״י שם ד״ה ״אף כל וכו׳ 47. רש״י שם ד״ה ״יצא ירקות שגדילין על מי שנה הבאה״
48. ״ומתעשרין לשנה הבאה״ גמ׳

than we would have reasoned.[30] The posuk of "באספך מגרנך ומיקבך" which speaks of "gathering" together with those species of wheat, grapes and olives, tells us that any produce which you gather that has the same common denominator as these species, then so also what determines them as produce of a particular year is the year in which they grow their first third.

The common denominator here is its form of water source. Wheat, grapes and olives grow from rain water alone and do not require irrigation.[31] Any other produce which grows only from rain water is also determined as being produce of a particular year by the year in which it grows its first third. This excludes vegetables (ירקות) which require irrigation as well as rain water,[32] and are therefore not included in this posuk of wheat, grapes and olives. The stage of maturity which determines to which year of produce they belong would logically be when they are picked (לקיטה), for that is the stage of peak maturity.

All other produce which does not grow on rain water alone will also follow the rule of לקיטה, unless there is a special posuk telling us otherwise, such as tree fruit[33] or the case of the species spoken of next.

---

(30) We see from the way Rabbi Akiva learns, that in order for the Torah to write a special posuk telling us that concerning this species their maturity to be called "produce" is earlier than one would reason, then we see that it is the Torah which assumes that normal maturity to be called "produce" is only when fully ripe i.e. at a time they are ready to be picked (לקיטה). Therefore even in Hilchos Shmittoh where vegetables have a din midorysa of being Shmittoh produce, what determines them midorysa as Shmittoh produce is if they are picked (לקיטה) during Shmittoh.[48a]

(31) Thus they are referred to as "גדלין על רוב מים".[48b]

(32) Thus they are referred to as "גדלין על כל מים".[48c]

(33) Where it was learned from the posuk concerning Orlah that the year in which it matures to the stage of חנטה determines that it is the produce of this year. N.B. This posuk only tells us a rule about tree fruit, therefore tells us nothing about species like vegetables etc.

48a. עיין קשה של תוס׳ ראש השנה יג: ד״ה "מתוך" ותירץ שני שם 48b. ראש השנה יד. 48c. ראש השנה שם

השרשה

The Mishna⁴⁹ tells us that as far as legumes such as אורז, דוחן
פרגים ושומשמן (rice, kinds of millet, and sesame) are concerned, then
what determines them as belonging to produce of a particular year
of Ma'aseros, and to the Shmittoh year, is if they take root (השרשה)
within this year. The Gemora⁵⁰ discusses that the reason for this is
because even though they are sown at the same time, nevertheless
unlike other species of produce they do not ripen at the same time
and therefore parts of the same crop get picked at different times,
and it could therefore happen that some would be picked before
Rosh Hashona and others picked after Rosh Hashona. Thereby if
לקיטה is what determines them as produce of a particular year then
one would have mixtures of old produce with new produce, a cause
of problems both for Ma'aseros and Shmittoh. These species,
however, when sown at the same time do take root at the same time,
therefore in considering their taking root as being the factor which
determines which year produce they belong would avoid this
problem of mixture. Therefore, as far as which year of Ma'aser they
belong the Rabbonon used השרשה as the determining factor.⁽³⁴⁾
Concerning Shmittoh this is also used as the determining factor,
however unlike the case of Ma'aseros it is not merely a suggestion by
the Rabbonon to avoid the problem of mixture, but it is the Torah
itself which dictates that this is the determining factor:⁵¹

The Torah⁵² concerning Shmittoh says "שש שנים תזרע שדך...ואספת
את תבואתה" "Six years you shall sow your field...and gather in its
produce". The very next posuk begins "ובשנה השביעית" "and in the
seventh year". This drosha seems to tell us that one is permitted to

---

(34) The obligation of separating Ma'aseros from these species being miderabbonon
allows the Rabbonon to exercise their rights to say that this should be the
determining factor.⁵⁰ᵃ

49. שביעית פ״ב מ״ז 50. ראש השנה יג: 50a. תוס׳ ראש השנה שם 51. לפי תירוץ שני בתוס׳ שם
בשם תורת כהנים 52. ויקרא כה: ג׳

gather (reap) the sixth year produce during Shmittoh even if they were sown in the sixth year and took root in the seventh year, yet the first posuk here has a contradictory implication i.e. it clearly says that in the sixth year one sows *and* reaps it, therefore implying that one is only permitted to reap it during the sixth year? This apparent contradiction is solved by saying that the Torah here means to say that only the produce which takes root during the sixth year may be reaped even during the seventh year,[35] but not that produce which is sown during the sixth year but only takes root during the seventh year.[36] The produce which the posuk is referring to, can only be to the species of legumes mentioned above, being that the problem of coming to mixtures only exists by them,[53] and is solved by saying that the factor determining them as Shmittoh produce is if they have their השרשה during this year.

The Gemora goes on to bring the statement of Shmuel that what determines even these species as to which year produce they belong is the year in which they reach גמר פרי.

The Rambam[54] paskens like Shmuel and understands that not only is Shmuel referring to the case of Ma'aseros where השרשה is merely the factor established by the Rabbonon, but even in the case of Shmittoh where the factor is dictated by the Torah.[55] Other Rishonim[56] understand that Shmuel's statement only refers to Ma'aseros, and what determines them as Shmittoh produce is if they have their השרשה during the Shmittoh year.

---

(35) Because having taken root in the sixth year they are considered produce of the sixth year.
(36) Because then they are produce of the seventh year being the Shmittoh year.

---

53. לפי פני יהושע על תוס׳ ר״ה יג: ד״ה ״ולכאורה״ 54. מעשר שני פ״א הל׳ ח׳. שמיטה ויובל פ״ד הל׳ י״א 55. עיין בכסף משנה שם 56. ר״ש שביעית פ״ב מ״ז

CHAPTER SIX

ספיחים (S'FICHIM)

1. Issur S'fichim—Midorysa or Miderabbonon?
Rabbi Akiva:

Rabbi Akiva's view is that except for tree fruit or the like, S'fichim which began growing during Shmittoh are forbidden to be eaten midorysa (termed "*issur S'fichim*"). He derives[1] this from the posuk which says[2] "וכי תאמרו מה נאכל בשנה השביעית הן לא נזרע ולא נאסף את תבואתנו" "and should you say 'what shall we eat during the seventh year, behold, we are not to sow and we are not to pick (gather in) our produce'". The question here[(1)] is—if there is no sowing, then obviously no produce will be available for picking? Rabbi Akiva learns that the posuk, in mentioning "we are not to pick our produce", must be referring to S'fichim. The posuk means to say the following: "what shall we eat during the seventh year, behold we are not to sow and we are not even to pick produce *which was not intentionally sown by us and grew by itself* (S'fichim)". Although sowing is forbidden, S'fichim will still grow and it is because this is also prohibited that the people will raise the question "what shall we *eat*?".

In addition, the fact that the posuk dealing with S'fichim says "what shall we *eat*?" implies that it is prohibited to eat S'fichim.[3]

The Rabbonon:

The Rabbonon understand that when the posuk says "לא נאסף" "we are not to pick our produce" it does in fact refer to produce

---

(1) The Toras Kohanim here is explained according to the way the Vilna Gaon has the text that rather than the Toras Kohanim explaining the question posed in the posuk, the Toras Kohanim is questioning the posuk itself.

1. ברייתא בת"כ ועי' פסחים נא: 2. ויקרא כה:כ 3. כן שמעתי מפי בעל משנת יוסף שליט"א ועי' בספרו ח"ד עמוד ט"ז שורה ראשון בתוספות אחרונים.

which has grown from intentional sowing, not S'fichim, and as far as the question this poses, that if no sowing is permitted then why is it necessary to prohibit picking? The Rabbonon answer[4] that it refers only to produce after the time of *biyur*. [2] The question of the Am Yisroel to HaShem[5] is "behold we are forbidden to sow, what we have gathered into storage, You tell us to dispose of it (biyur), therefore what shall we eat after this time of disposal?"

These Rabbonon, however, are of the view that there is a Rabbinical decree forbidding the eating of S'fichim. This decree was made on account of the following problem:[6]

Being that the Torah permits the eating of wild vegetables during Shmittoh, a Jew who does not adhere to the halochos of Shmittoh might secretly sow vegetables during Shmittoh, and will claim that they grew wild. In order to prevent this, the Chachomim decreed that all vegetables which grow in the field of a Jew are fobidden to be eaten.

There is no decree prohibiting produce which grew in the field of a non-Jew, this being because a non-Jew himself, is not commanded to observe the halochos of Shmittoh and therefore the Rabbonon did not extend *issur S'fichim* to his vegetables.[7] As far as the fear that a Jew may sow there, the non-Jew would not permit it.[8] As far as tree fruit is concerned, even though they are S'fichim,[9] they have no *issur S'fichim*. All trees old enough to bear fruits ready for eating are already existing before Shmittoh. In addition, no immediate benefit is accrued from planting a tree, since it takes some time before a tree bears fruit. Vegetables, on the other hand, grow quickly and there is reason to fear that people will violate Shmittoh by planting them.

---

(2) When a type of food no longer exists in the field, available to all, no stocks of it can be kept. Divesting oneself of ownership of these products is called "the time of biyur" and of course will vary with each type of produce.

4. לפי ת״כ 5. מהרש״ל פסחים נא: 6. רמב״ם שמיטה ויובל פ״ד הל׳ ב׳ 7. רמב״ם שם הל׳ כ״ט 8. ספר שמיטה כהלכתה פ״ב ט״ו בביאור שם. 9. רמב״ם שם הל׳ ג׳ והל׳ י׳

Therefore the issur midrabbonon of S'fichim was not extended to tree fruit, but only to vegetables and the like.

The Chachomim bring an *Asmachta* for their decree on S'fichim from the posuk[10] ״את ספיח קצירך לא תקצור״ "the s'fiach of your harvest you shall not pick". All agree that this posuk prohibits harvesting Shmittoh crops in the regular manner (but permitted if harvested in an unusual manner[3]), nevertheless the Chachomim use it as an *Asmachta* to say that S'fichim must not be harvested at all,[11] (therefore they cannot be eaten).

As well as there being a dispute between Rabbi Akiva and the Rabbonon as to whether *issur S'fichim* is midorysa (Rabbi Akiva) or miderabbonon (Rabbonon), there is also a dispute between Rabbi Shimon and the Rabbonon whether *kruv* (kale) is forbidden as S'fichim miderabbonon in addition to all vegetables (see below no. 2).

Some Rishonim[12] learn that the Rabbonon who dispute Rabbi Akiva are not the same Rabbonon who dispute Rabbi Shimon. The Rabbonon who dispute Rabbi Shimon agree with him that the halocha is like Rabbi Akiva, merely disagreeing as to whether Rabbi Akiva extends the *issur S'fichim* to *kruv*.

Consequently, these Rishonim pasken that the halocha is like Rabbi Akiva, being that the Rabbonon who argue with Rabbi Shimon agree that S'fichim itself is midorysa, giving Rabbi Akiva the benefit of their majority opinion. However the Rambam[13] paskens that the halocha is like the Rabbonon that the *issur S'fichim* is miderabbonon, his reason being that he understands that the "Rabbonon" who dispute Rabbi Shimon are the same Rabbonon who dispute Rabbi Akiva,[14] with the halocha following the majority, the Rabbonon.

(3) See Chapter Seven.

10. ויקרא כה: ה, לפי ת״כ 11. תורה־תמימה על הפסוק סוף ס״ק ט״ו 12. סמ״ג ל״ת רס״ח, היראים סימן קנ״ח 13. שם הל׳ ב׳ 14. עי׳ משנת יוסף פ:ט מ״א בשיטות המפרשים ס״ק א׳

2. Tree Fruit and Kruv

This prohibition midorysa to eat S'fichim which Rabbi Akiva derived from the posuk הן לא נזרע (see above no. 1) does not include S'fichim of tree fruit because[15] by the Torah here having mentioned the expression of sowing ("לא נזרע") in juxtaposition with picking produce (ולא נאסף), which refers to S'fichim, it thereby informs us that only those S'fichim which have grown (and are completed for the present harvest) from a *sown* seed are included in the issur Torah here, thereby excluding S'fichim of tree fruit, since they do not grow from the sown tree seed but grow from the *branches* of the tree.[4]

There is a species of vegetable, "כרוב" (kruv, in English—kale) which unlike other vegetables, its edible part grows from branches.[16] Therefore like tree fruit it does not come under the Torah prohibition of S'fichim.[5] Kruv, however, is similar in certain ways to a vegetable, and to permit kruv could lead to the mistaken impression that other vegetables are also permitted.[17] There is a dispute amongst the Tannoim[18] whether even according to Rabbi Akiva there is a Rabbinical prohibition on kruv which grows during the Shmittoh year.[18a] Rabbi Shimon says there is no such prohibition. According to the Rabbonon there is.

The fruit of trees however do not have these similarities and therefore there is no worry that one might come to such confusion.

There are circumstances, however, where even according to Rabbi Shimon kruv has a stringency over and above other S'fichim. In the case of a kruv which has been sown and has completed its

---

(4) Although they are permissible to be eaten nevertheless being that they have had חנטה (see Chapter Five) during Shmittoh they have Kedushas Shviyis (ibid), and therefore have halochic limitations, such as it being prohibited to do business with them.
(5) However they have Kedushas Shviyis and therefore have halochic limitations such as it being prohibited to do business with them.

15. לפי תוס׳ פסחים נא: ד״ה ״כל״ וז״ל ״דלא אסרה תורה אלא ספיחים דומיא דזריעה דכתיב ״הן לא נזרע״ ועי׳ ברש״י שם ד״ה ״שאין כיוצא בהן בירק השדה״. 16. רש״י פסחים נא: ד״ה ״שאין כיוצא בהן בירק השדה״. 17. רש״י שם ד״ה ״גזרינן ספיחי כרוב אטו ספיחין דעלמא״ 18. פסחים נא: 18a על פי פשט של הר״ש פ״ט מ״א ועי׳ בתוס׳ רע״ק אות מ״א

growth (גמר פרי) during the sixth year then it is considered sixth year produce even if it is picked (לקיטה) during Shmittoh,[6] therefore it has no *Kedushas Shviyis* that it should have any of the prohibitions on it, such as doing business (סחורה) with it. However, on account of the fact that kruv can grow additional leaves and it is difficult to distinguish between its old leaves and its newly grown leaves, therefore it could happen that even after its גמר פרי in the sixth year, one could pick leaves from it thinking they are the old leaves[7] yet which grew during the Shmittoh year thereby having *Kedushas Shviyis* and therefore having halochic limitations such as a prohibition of doing business with them.[19] On account of the possibility of making such a mistake, Rabbi Shimon prohibits doing business even with a kruv which grew during the sixth year.[8] The Rabbonon say that there is this decree on other S'fichim as well, because if not so then one might in confusion think that it is permitted to do business with kruv.[20] The Chazon Ish[21] writes that the halocha is like the Rabbonon.[9]

Regarding tree fruit (or kruv) there is no *Torah* prohibition of S'fichim neither according to Rabbi Shimon nor according to the Rabbonon.[10]

Consequently, when the Torah [22] informs us והיתה שבת הארץ לכם לאכלה ''and the resting of the land shall be yours to eat'' it refers to S'fichim like tree fruit[23] and kruv.

(6)   Even if picked during Shmittoh, the year to which a vegetable belongs is determined by גמר פרי (see Chapter Five).
(7)   Referred to as the ''אמהות'' (lit: mothers).
(8)   The part which grew during the sixth year is of course permitted to be eaten.
(9)   Therefore even S'fichim which have their גמר פרי during the sixth year, miderabbonon have Kedushas Shviyis so that it is forbidden to do business with them. It is, however, permitted to eat them.
(10)   However the halocha is like the Rabbonon, that miderabbonon kruv are forbidden to be eaten.[21a]

19. על פי ר״ש שם ועי׳ תוס׳ רע״ק שם 20. וכולה חדא גזירה היא, כן כתב בתורת שביעית עמוד רל״ח 21. שביעית סימן ז׳ ס״ק ט״ז ד״ה ״אורז״ (בתרא) וסימן ט׳ סוף ס״ק א. 21a. ע״י משנת יוסף פ״ט מ״א שיטות המפרשים סוף ס״ק ב׳ 22. ויקרא כה: ו עם פירש״י 23. תוס׳ רי״ד פסחים נא: ועי׳ במהר״ם לובלין פסחים שם.

3. Only S'fichim which are sown during Shmittoh can become forbidden midorysa

As mentioned above, the posuk from which Rabbi Akiva derives the Torah prohibition to eat S'fichim uses the expression of sowing (לא נזרע) adjacent to the words expressing S'fichim (ולא נאסף), therefore[24] by way of *hekesh* it can now also be understood that when there is a prohibition to sow (לא נזרע) there is also a prohibition to gather, (the S'fichim) (ולא נאסף). The prohibition to sow takes effect at the beginning of Shmittoh. This is derived from[25] "ובשנה השביעית...שדך לא תזרע" "but in the seventh year...your field you shall not sow", meaning that only from when Shmittoh *begins* is there an issur to sow.

The *hekesh* of S'fichim to sowing tells us that the *issur S'fichim* also is only on produce which is sown in the seventh year.[(11)]

4. The time when the issur S'fichim takes effect

Rashi[26] learns that Rabbi Akiva's view that midorysa the prohibition to eat S'fichim only applies *after* the time of disposal (*biyur*).[(12)] Tosfos[27] and other Rishonim[28] ask, since there already exists a prohibition to eat produce after the time of *biyur*,[29] then prohibiting S'fichim at this time is unnecessary?

Tosfos and the other Rishonim therefore learn that the prohibition to eat S'fichim which Rabbi Akiva refers to always exists from the beginning of the crops growth.

---

(11) If they are sown and begin growing in the sixth year they are permissible to be eaten even though they reach their full development (גמר פרי) during Shmittoh. They are considered seventh year produce and have Kedushas Shviyis (see Chapter Five). If they have their גמר פרי during the sixth year then they are sixth year produce and have no Kedushas Shviyis midorysa (see footnote (9)).

(12) See footnote (2).

24. על פי ר"ש שם י"ח שורות מסוף דבריו ופשט בדרשה שמעתי מפי בעל המחבר משנת יוסף שליט"א. 25. ויקרא כה:ד. 26. פסחים נא: ד"ה "ונטל ספיחי כרוב". 27. פסחים נא: ד"ה "כל" 28. ר"ש שביעית/פ"ט מ"א ובת"כ בהר א', ג' ורמב"ם שם הל' ב'. 29. ויקרא כה:ז

The Chachomim did not extend their decree to species which the majority of people do not cultivate, such as rue (פיגם) or amaranth (ירבוז)[30] since there is little worry that one who transgresses the Shmittoh laws will be sowing such species. The Chazon Ish[31] writes that should the majority of the population begin cultivating species that formerly usually grew wild, or stop cultivating previously cultivated species, then the decree will follow the new circumstances, covering newly cultivated species and permitting species no longer cultivated.

5. The Four Fields

There are four kinds of fields where S'fichim growing in them are not even forbidden miderabbonon[32] since it is not likely that they would be cultivated, or cultivation would actually be against the owner's best interest.

1) שדה בור A field where difficult conditions of the area[33] make it unlikely that people would sow in it.

2) שדה ניר A field which has yet to be ploughed, therefore needs to be free of plantation.[34] Therefore it is not in the owner's interest to plant before ploughing.

3) שדה כרם A vineyard. One would not intentionally sow vegetables in his vineyard, since this would make it כלאים, and people would not buy his grapes.

4) שדה זרע A field which is sown with תלתן (fenogrec). Any other species sown there would spoil the תלתן, thus any other growth there would only be from what was sown by itself.

30. רמב״ם שם הל׳ ג׳. 31. שביעית סימן ט׳ ס״ק י״ז ד״ה ״ויש לעי׳ בירקות״ 32. רמב״ם שם הל׳ ד׳
על פי ירושלמי בבא בתרא פ״ח הל׳ א׳. 33. חזו״א שביעית סימן י׳ ס״ק א׳ 34. פני משה בירושלמי
שם

6. According to the p'sak that issur S'fichim is miderabbonon, when do they have to grow in order to have this issur applying to them?

What determines which year vegetables belong to is the year they reach their full development גמר פרי, and the term לקיטה is usually used because when they reach גמר פרי they usually are picked.35(13) However, after this stage of גמר פרי sometimes they may be left to continue to grow until they eventually stop growing, and then they are picked. Therefore it is possible to have two different times when they can be picked (לקיטה), גמר פרי and after גמר פרי. The Rambam36 paskens that if S'fichim reached the first גמר פרי during the sixth year but a bit of further growth occurs during Shmittoh, then being that the time of the לקיטה for the second and final גמר פרי is during Shmittoh they have an *issur S'fichim*.(14) If, however during the sixth year they attained both stages of גמר פרי37(15) even it they are picked (לקיטה) during Shmittoh they have no *issur S'fichim*. לקיטה during Shmittoh does however give them *Kedushas Shviyis*.(16)

The Chazon Ish38 paskens like those Rishonim who say that the *issur S'fichim* miderabbonon is only on that which begins its growth during Shmittoh but not if it begins growing during the sixth year even though it continues into Shmittoh.

(13) Most vegetables are edible the moment they sprout35a therefore their גמר פרי is determined by what size they are when they are usually picked (לקיטה).

(14) In other words as long as their second and final גמר פרי occurs during Shmittoh they have *issur s'fichim*, and certainly so when their first גמר פרי occurs during Shmittoh they have *issur s'fichim*.

(15) Their second and final גמר פרי also occurs during the sixth year.

(16) Kedushas Shviyis is determined by לקיטה occuring during Shmittoh despite the fact that it *could have* been picked (לקיטה) during the sixth year.

35. תוס' ר"ה יג: ד"ה "אחר" 35a. עיין פיה"מ לר"מ מעשרות פ"א מ"א 36. שם הל' י"ב ועי' בחזו"א שביעית סימן ט' ס"ק ב"ג 37. נגמר כולו בששית לגמרי 38. שביעית סימן ט' ס"ק י"ז

7. Defining the beginnings of growth

The Chazon Ish[39] is of the opinion that even vegetables like cucumbers, where the cucumber is preceded by a leafy growth, nevertheless this growth alone can be considered grown during the sixth year and is permissible to be eaten, even though the cucumber itself has not yet emerged. Others[40] are of the opinion that only when the cucumber has reached the stage of growth of עונת המעשרות[17] during the sixth year is it permissible to be eaten. The minhag follows the view of the Chazon Ish.[41]

The *issur S'fichim* only applies to תבואה (grain) and some קטניות (legumes) if they reach the first third of their growth during Shmittoh.[42] A suggested reason brought[43] for why the measure of what is considered growth for *issur S'fichim* is different for תבואה than for vegetables is because with regard to הבאת שליש as well as being that which determines which year the תבואה is considered a produce of, we have proof that it also determines when it is considered as having "grown" i.e. in the case where תבואה reaches a third of its growth while in the possession of a non-Jew it is exempt from חיוב הפרשת תרו"מ since it is considered as having *grown* in the domain of a non-Jew.[44] Thus in fixing the time when the *issur S'fichim* applies to תבואה the Chachomim used this as their gauge (i.e. they fixed it כעין דאורייתא[18]). However concerning vegetables we see no proof that לקיטה determines when it is considered as having reached a minimal growth but only determines which year produce it belongs to. Therefore the Chachomim gave their own measure for when the *issur S'fichim* applies to them i.e. when it *begins* to grow during Shmittoh.

(17) The stage of development when it can be considered a vegetable, before it has גמר פרי but after the green growth.
(18) The Chachomim, in making their decrees, tried to pattern them after a din dorysa to which they were similar.

39. עי' משנת יוסף פ"ט מ"א שיטות המפרשים 40. משנת יוסף שם 41. משנת יוסף שם 42. ירושלמי מעשרות פ"ה הל' ב' תוספתא שביעית פ"ב אות י' ועי' ברמב"ם שם הל' י' וברדב"ז שם. 43. עי' במקדש דוד נט,ג. 44. ירושלמי מעשרות פ"ה הל' ב'

8. May one benefit from S'fichim?

According to Rabbi Akiva that the *issur S'fichim* is midorysa, then the only prohibition is an issur to eat them. Since this is the whole drosha of the posuk.[45]

According to the Rabbonon, however, that the *issur S'fichim* is miderabbonon, then it appears that they also forbade one to have any personal use from S'fichim.[46]

9. Until when there is a worry that produce may have an issur S'fichim

Produce classified under the *issur S'fichim* never becomes permissible. This applies not only to those S'fichim which began growing and are picked during Shmittoh (true seventh year produce), but also to those S'fichim which grow during Shmittoh but are picked in the eighth year (eighth year produce).[47] The Chachomim[48] forbade even these S'fichim in order to prevent people who might pick S'fichim during Shmittoh (Shmittoh produce which never becomes permitted) but store them until the eighth year and claim they were picked during the eighth year (so that he can sell them). This eighth year *issur S'fichim* is only forbidden until the time that each particular species could have already grown and ripened had it been sown after Rosh Hashona of the eighth year.[19] This is termed as having been "עשו כיוצא בהם". A list of dates are therefore published by Bais Din to inform people of these times.

---

(19) On account of this any s'fiach of this species can be attributed to having been sown after Rosh Hashona, or even if it began growing in Shmittoh, by this time most of the plant would have had its growth in the eighth year and thus nullified the issur within it.[48a]

---

45. שער המלך שמיטה ויובל ד'. ב' ועי' במשנת יוסף ח"ד עמוד ט"ז בתוספות אחרונים. 46. על פי
משמעות חזו"א   בסדר השביעית סעיף א' ובסימן י"ג ס"ק ט"ז ד"ה "ריש" עי' במשנת יוסף ח"ד
עמוד י"ח תוספות אחרונים 47. רמב"ם שם הל' ט"ו 48. ר"ש שביעית פ"ו מ"ד ועיין בחזו"א
שביעית סימן ט' ס"ק י"ג 48a. פיה"מ לר"מ ור"ש שביעית פ"ו מ"ד

The Gemora[49] states that S'fichim are forbidden from Rosh Hashona (of the eighth year) until Chanukah (of the eighth year). This means to say[50] that even if there are species of S'fichim which are not yet עשו כיוצא בהם by the time of Chanukah, nevertheless it is permitted to eat them, since there is no worry that in permitting them at this time one might pick S'fichim in Shmittoh and store them for such a long time. This is how the Rambam[51] paskens.

49. ירושלמי דמאי פ״ב הל׳ א׳ (דף ח:) 50. לפי חזו״א שם 51. שם הל׳ ו׳

CHAPTER SEVEN

GUARDED (משומר) AND WORKED (ונעבד) PRODUCE

1. The source for the concept of משומר

The source for the concept of משומר is a *Toras Kohanim*. [1] In order to facilitate the understanding and review of this fairly complex subject, a chart summarizing how the various Rishonim and Achronim understand this *Toras Kohanim* is presented at the end of this section.

The *Toras Kohanim* is being presented here as containing two basic components. labeled A and B.

The *Toras Kohanim*[1] reads as follows:

A. *The Posuk*—ואת ענבי נזיריך לא תבצור

The Drosha—מן השומר בארץ אין אתה בוצר אבל אתה בוצר מן המופקר

B. *The Posuk*—לא תבצור

The Drosha—לא תבצור כדרך הבוצרים

To further explain these two components of the *Toras Kohanim*:

A. The Torah says "ואת ענבי נזיריך לא תבצור" "and the grapes which you have set aside for yourselves[2] you shall not pick". The *Toras Kohanim* derives from this posuk that "you cannot pick[3] what you have guarded (for yourself), but you pick what you have left ownerless".

---

(1) A collection of droshos Chazal on ויקרא.

(2) This is the interpretation of the word "נזיריך"[1a] i.e barred and kept away from people. This speaks of produce which was sown in the sixth year.[1b]

(3) Although the Toras Kohanim speaks of בוצר, picking grapes, it also refers to קוצר, reaping grain and legumes.[1c]

---

1. פרשת בהר פ״א, ג. 1a. תוס׳ סוכה לט: ד״ה ״בד״א״ 1b. ירושלמי שביעית פ״ח הל׳ ו׳ ״אם אינו ענין לספיחי איסור תנהו לספיחי היתר״ 1c. ירושלמי שם

B. The derivation from the words "לא תבצור" "You shall not pick" at the end of this posuk is that "you may not pick in the manner of the pickers but only with a deviation."

These words, which are the source for the concept of משומר, are disputed among the Rishonim. The basic point of dispute is whether the deviation spoken of in B speaks of משומר or מופקר.

Tosfos, Rabbeinu Tam, other Rishonim and the Vilna Gaon

Tosfos[2] mentions drosha A and says that the *Toras Kohanim* here cannot be referring to what its simple meaning implies, that בוצר, picking משומר produce is forbidden and picking מופקר produce is permitted. Such a statement cannot be true since the Torah[3] says "לא תקצור" "you shall not reap", referring both to משומר and מופקר produce (being that the Torah here makes no special mention excluding הפקר) and בוצר is a Toldah of קוצר. Therefore "לא תקצור" tells us that it is fobidden to be בוצר even הפקר produce.[4] We are therefore forced to say that drosha A cannot be saying that picking מופקר produce is permitted.[5] Rather what the *Toras Kohanim* means to say is that if one transgressed and picked משומר produce its *consumption* is forbidden[6] but if one picked מופקר produce its consumption is permitted.

Accordingly Tosfos will learn that drosha B comes to add that concerning מופקר produce if one deviates in the way he picks it, then this form of picking is completely permitted.[7]

(4) Tosfos here is clearly learning that even Toldos (of the four melochos זורע, זומר בוצר, קוצר, see Chapter Three) are forbidden midorysa during Shmittoh, therefore understanding the Gemora in מועד קטן differently from Rashi (ibid).

(5) Without a deviation from the normal way, see below.

(6) It is likely that the Toras Kohanim derives this from the posuk "והיתה שבת הארץ וכו'" (to be explained). The Ravad,[3a] in agreement with Tosfos, states here that consumption of משומר produce is forbidden, clearly saying that drosha A is not precise in its wording[3b] and means to say that there is a prohibition to consume משומר produce (בוצר מן המופקר), מן השומר בארץ אין אתה בוצר אבל אתה, the prohibition of consuming משומר produce being learned from the posuk והיתה שבת הארץ.

(7) Picking משומר produce is forbidden even with a deviation.

2. בבא מציעא נח. ד"ה "לשמור" לפי המהרש"א. 3. ויקרא כה: ה 3a. בת"כ שם 3b. נראה לי שאין זה המדרש נדרש מזה הפסוק וכו'

Rabbeinu Tam,[4] other Rishonim[5] and the Vilna Gaon[6] are of the same opinion that consumption of משומר produce is forbidden,[8] their source being from this *Toras Kohanim*.[9]

Rashi, other Rishonim

Rashi[7] understands that it is forbidden to pick משומר produce but if one is מפקיר it, then it is permitted to pick it in the normal way even without deviation.[7] Rashi is of the opinion[8] that although while produce is in the state of משומר its consumption is forbidden[10] nevertheless if it is declared הפקר it becomes permitted.[11][12]

(8) There is, however, no prohibition of having any other benefit from it.[6a]

(9) The Chazon Ish[6b] suggests the possibility that Rabbeinu Tam (and the other Rishonim in agreement with Rabbeinu Tam) is of the view that if while the fruits are still attached to the tree one regrets having been שומר them and he is מפקיר them, then if the majority of its growth continues while in this הפקר state their consumption becomes permitted (the majority of הפקר nullifying the minority of משומר). Only when this is not the case does Rabbeinu Tam understand that their consumption is forbidden.

(10) Derived from והיתה שבת הארץ[8a] (to be explained).

(11) Understanding that the concept of "משומר" is not an *act* which creates a prohibition. Rather it is a *state*. i.e. The Torah says that produce in a *state* of משומר is forbidden to be eaten (since only הפקר may be consumed).

Therefore when the state of משומר is removed it is permitted to eat. Rabbeinu Tam and the other Rishonim understand that the Torah is saying that the *act* of being שומר produce creates a prohibition of consumption, therefore even if the שמירה is removed, their consumption remains prohibited, unless one is מפקיר them while still attached to the tree and the majority of their growth is in this state in such a case the growth in הפקר nullifies the minority of that which is prohibited (see footnote (9)). Thus Rashi and Rabbeinu Tam agree that consumption of משומר produce is forbidden where the majority of the fruit grew while משומר, and one is not מפקיר it. They agree that consumption is permitted where the majority of the fruit grew after having been מפקיר it. They disagree where there is only a minority of growth after having been מפקיר it.

(12) Those living in Bnei Brak who have the custom to permit the eating of משומר produce should therefore have to מפקיר such produce before consuming it. Such produce in Bnei Brak is under the jurisdiction of Bais Din (termed *Otzer Bais Din*) this creates a situation where the consumer himself does not have to carry out the procedure of making it הפקר[8b]

4. תוס׳ סוכה לט:ד״ה ״בד״א״ 5. רבותיו של רש״י יבמות קכב. ריש ד״ה ״של עזיקה״ (עי׳ תוס׳ סוכה שם שזה רבותיו של רש״י) תוס׳ ראש השנה ט. ד״ה ״וקוצר״ (בתרא) ובעל המאור סוכה שם. ראב״ד על ת״כ שם 6. שנות אליהו שביעית פ״ח מ״י ובביאורו על ת״כ 6a. ערוך לנר סוכה לט: על תוס׳ שם 6b. שביעית סימן י׳ ס״ק ה׳ וע״ע בסימן י״ב ס״ק ד׳ 7. ויקרא כה:ה לפי הרמב״ן 8. לפי הרמב״ן שם ומזרחי שם והקרבן אהרן בת״כ 8a. עיין מזרחי שם 8b. כן שמעתי מבעל משנת יוסף שליט״א

Consequently Rashi will understand that drosha A does not speak of a prohibition of consuming משומר produce etc but rather speaks of the act of picking, prohibited in משומר, permitted in מופקר, drosha B adding that with a deviation it is permitted in משומר. מופקר produce can be reaped as normal. Several other Rishonim[9] are in agreement with Rashi.

Ramban

It is clear, however, that although the Ramban[10] agrees that consumption of משומר produce can become permitted, nevertheless his understanding of the droshos in the *Toras Kohanim* is different. This stems from his own understanding of the word "נזיריך". That is,[11] the word "נזיריך" "your barring" of "ואת ענבי נזיריך לא תבצור" according to the Ramban means that you keep yourself away from doing any work to Shmittoh produce, such as pruning etc, the fact that the owner does no work to it is a sign that he has indeed relinquished ownership (it is מופקר produce). Even here the Torah says "לא תבצור", one may not pick in the usual manner.[13]

Therefore the Ramban says that the understanding of the *Toras Kohanim* is that "נזיריך לא תבצור" means "you shall not act with Shmittoh produce as a בעל הבית does but only as an עני does. As a בעל הבית you do two things: 1) You pick what is *closed* off, exclusively yours, i.e. משומר, 2) You pick it in your normal way with the proper tools, and process it in its special place. Thus the Torah here tells us that during Shmittoh you must rather reap or pick produce like a poor man usually does i.e 1) From הפקר and not *at all* from משומר; this is expressed in drosha A. 2) When reaping or picking from הפקר it is not done with the usual tools and not

_____

(13) Being that concerning Shmittoh produce the Torah says "לאכלה" "to eat it" therefore there cannot be an entire   prohibition to reap or pick it.[11a]

9. תוס' סוכה לט: שם ובמנחות פד. שם ד"ה "שומרי" ר"ש שביעית פ"ח מ"ו,חינוך מצוה שכ"ט 10. שם
11. לפי חינוך שם 11a. עי' פיה"מ לר"מ שביעית פ"ח מ"ו

processed in a special place; this is expressed in B.(14)

The Ramban, however, is of the opinion that the need to reap or pick מופקר produce with a deviation is miderabbonon, and was instituted in order to prevent one from being שומר the produce, the posuk here is their *Asmachta*.12

Questions against both views:

There are two questions posed13 against the view of Rabbeinu Tam that the consumption of משומר produce is forbidden:

1) Since drosha A speaks of משומר produce, then what immediately follows should be a continuation of this subject informing us that the prohibition to pick משומר produce is only in the usual manner but permitted with a deviation.

2) The second question is from the following Gemora:

Money paid for Shmittoh produce receives *Kedushas Shviyis*(15) and may only be spent on food and drink. It therefore may not be given to an *Am Ha'oretz* who may spend it on other things.14 The Gemora brings a Beraisa that in payment for Shmittoh produce one may give an *Am Ha'oretz* money equivalent to the cost of three meals. This is because the *Am Ha'oretz*, needing the money for food will spend it on such and not use it to buy non-food items.15 The Gemora, however, stipulates that one may only give him this money if one saw that the fruit being purchased was taken from an ownerless field, but not if taken from משומר. Rashi understands that this is because in giving him money for משומר produce one will encourage him to continue to keep possession of the fruit,16 such

---

(14) In learning that drosha A of the Toras Kohanim speaks of the *act* of picking, therefore we understand why his opinion is in agreement with Rashi that consumption of משומר produce can become permitted.
(15) See Chapter Five.[1*]

12. חזו"א שביעית סימן י"ב ס"ק ד' וה'. 13. תוס' סוכה לט: ד"ה "בד"א" 14 תוס' סוכה שם ד"ה "שאין" 15. רש"י שם כדי חייב 16. ריטב"א שם מסעייה עוברי עבירה

possession being forbidden during Shmittoh since the fruit must be genuinely ownerless. Rashi only discussing this problem keeps within his view that the consumption of the משומר produce itself is permitted.[17] Rabbeinu Tam[18] on the other hand keeping within his view understands that the reason why one may not buy the fruit is because its consumption is forbidden. Tosfos, however, asks his second question on Rabbeinu Tam: How can Rabbeinu Tam say that the produce is forbidden to be eaten? Surely the Gemora here is merely prohibiting the *purchase* of the food, implying that it could be eaten, for were it forbidden to be eaten, there would be no need to prohibit its purchase, since food forbidden to be eaten would anyway not be bought?

On the other hand there are two questions[19] which are posed against the view of Rashi and the other Rishonim:

1) Immediately preceding drosha A the *Toras Kohanim* derives from the beginning of the posuk of "ואת ענבי נזיריך וכו'" that S'fichim[16] are forbidden to be eaten ("את ספיח קצירך לא תקצור"), therefore it is likely that what follows also discusses something forbidden to be eaten.

2) The last part of drosha B which discusses the various forms of picking with a deviation is a quote from a Mishna[20] which does not specify that it speaks in connection with משומר produce. It may be assumed to be discussing הפקר, since this is the usual state of Shmittoh produce.

---

(16) See Chapter Six.

17. ריטב"א שם 18. תוס' שם ד"ה "בד"א". 19. תוס' שם ור"ש בת"כ פרשת בהר פ"א ס"ק ג' ד"ה "אלא על מופקרין" (בהמשך) 20. שביעית פ"ח מ"ו

If a non-Jew is שומר **his produce does it have a halocha of** משומר **produce?**

A Beraisa states[21] "If a non-Jew is selling fruit and claims that the fruit is ערלה,[17] or is from עזיקה (to be explained) or is נטע רבעי,[18] he is not believed since his intention in saying this is merely because he wants to make a sale (these different kinds of fruit have a special quality.[22])".

The Ba'al HaM'or[23] understanding that "עזיקה" refers to an area where produce is משומר, brings this Beraisa as a proof that the consumption of משומר produce is forbidden. The Ravad[24] understands that in having brought this particular case involving a non-Jew to prove that the consumption of משומר produce is forbidden, then the Ba'al HaM'or is learning that even produce of a non-Jew which was not left ownerless, is forbidden to a Jew until it indeed becomes ownerless.[19] The Ravad himself disputes this.[20]

The Rambam in his Commentary on the Mishna[25] mentions the drosha of the *Toras Kohanim* that picking must be done with a deviation, he does not discuss whether this speaks of משומר or מופקר.

(17) See Chapter Four.[1*]
(18) ibid.
(19) In other words, understanding that it is the mere שמירה of Shmittoh produce which gives it a prohibition of consumption.
(20) Understanding that only שמירה which is prohibited (שמירה of a Jew) gives Shmittoh produce a prohibition of consumption.

21. יבמות קכב 22. רש"י שם 23. סוכה לט: 24. בהשגות שם 25. שביעית פ"ח מ"ו

	A	B	
	חורש כ'ביס		
	ואם תאמר כזוב יאך אתה אומר כל המסמר מן ומסמר כזוב	ונבצרים אל ונבצרו בורד	ואסר אביבוה
ניב"א ו'"ה וקב"אה	הפקר חורש ובכ'ילה ובאחר אמר ובכ'ילה	חורש בבכ'רה ואאין חורש בבכ'אואפך	בן
וקב"ן	הפקר בכבאקל אמר	חורש בבכ'רה ואאין חורש בבכ'אואפך	אל
ומ'"י וקב"אה	הפקר בכבאקל אמר	חורש בבכ'רה ואאין חורש בבכ'אואפך	אל

2. What is the source that produce worked (נעבד) and grown during Shmittoh is forbidden?

The Gemora[26] asks whether it is permitted to sow barley seeds during Shmittoh if there are no barley S'fichim[21] available to be brought for the Omer.[22] The Gemora answers that it would be similar to "קומץ על השיירים שאינם נאכלין", if a meal offering (קרבן מנחה) consists of grain which is prohibited to eat, then even the קומץ (handful) which is burned on the Mizbei'ach is invalid, since the remainder cannot be eaten. This would also hold true for an Omer brought from grain sown during Shmittoh, since the remainder cannot be eaten, the קומץ itself is not valid.

The Gemora is clearly implying that נעבד (produce worked with during Shmittoh) is forbidden to be eaten. One must say that this has also informed us that it is midorysa, being that there is no שבות במקדש[27] i.e. a prohibition miderabbonon would have been permitted in the Mikdosh.

The ערוך

The Aruch[28] and other Rishonim[29] have a different source that the consumption of נעבד produce is prohibited. The word "עזיקה" in the Beraisa mentioned above concerning the non-Jew selling fruits, according to the Aruch refers to Shmittoh produce which grew from ploughing during Shmittoh.[23] The intention of the non-Jew in saying that the fruits he is selling is "של עזיקה" is that they come from well ploughed land (therefore being good quality produce) and not

---

(21) Seeds grown without having been sown by man, see Chapter Six.

(22) Just like reaping the Omer takes precedence over Shabbos (see "Shmittoh in Depth" Chapter Four no. 1), perhaps sowing it also supercedes the prohibition to sow during Shmittoh.[26a]

(23) "עזיקה" referring to "ploughing", similar to "ויעזקהו ויסקלהו ויטעהו" "and he *ploughed* it, and cleared away its stones, and planted it".[29a]

---

26. ירושלמי שקלים פ״ד הל׳ א׳ 26a. פני משה שם 27. עי׳ ספר הלכות שביעית סימן ג׳, א׳ בביאור הלכה. 28. ערך עזק הובא בתוס׳ מנחות פד. ד״ה ״שומרי״ 29. תוס׳ מנחות שם וחידושי הרשב״א יבמות קכב. בשם ״פירוש אחר״ 29a. ישעיה ה:ב

from an unkept field. Consequently the Beraisa implies that produce growing from נעבד is forbidden to be eaten, since we permit the produce only because we do not believe the non-Jew, who is making this claim only to present his produce as being of a better quality.

The ר"ש

The *Toras Kohanim*[30] quoting the posuk[31] "והיתה שבת הארץ לכם לאכלה" "And the resting of (the produce) of the land shall be to you for eating" makes a drosha from here "מן השבות בארץ אתה אוכל ואין אתה אוכל מן השומר" "you may only eat produce which has "rested", but not from משומר produce".[24] The *Toras Kohanim* then says that Bais Shammai understand according to this drosha that in a case of נטייבה i.e. ploughing a field during Shmittoh (נעבד) then the consumption of produce resulting from this is forbidden.[25] The Rash[32] explains Bais Shammai to be understanding that when produce is נעבד it is considered a form of משומר[26], so much so that

(24) According to Rashi and the Rishonim who understand that consumption of משומר produce is permitted, they nevertheless learn from here that while in the state of משומר consumption of it is forbidden.[31a] According to Rabbeinu Tam and the Rishonim who already understand from the drosha derived from "ואת ענבי נזירך לא תבצור" that consumption of משומר produce is forbidden, it is suggested that what they derive from the drosha והיתה שבת הארץ is that there is also a *positive* commandment not to consume משומר produce.

(25) Some learn[31b] that the word "נטייבה" means ploughing the same area of land a second time over, therefore only produce resulting from this is forbidden to eat according to Bais Shammai. The first ploughing having been permitted on account of המלכות אונסת, if one did not plough his field it would be forcefully taken away from him by the Gentile rule,[31c] therefore under such conditions the Chachomim were able to lift the prohibition of חורש. Another opinion[31d] however is that it speaks of a regular period, with no royal decree, and נטייבה refers to ploughing a field just once over which is forbidden. Bais Shammai understand that from such נעבד consumption of the produce resulting from it is forbidden, and this is how the Rash learns.[31c] However it is unclear if the prohibition of consumption which Bais Shammai discusses is midorysa or miderabbonon.[31f]

(26) Since the beginning of the drosha discusses משומר.

30. פרשת בהר פרק א' אות ה' 31. ויקרא כה:ו 31a. ירושלמי פ"ד הל' ב' לפי מ"ד אחר 31c. ראב"ד הובא ברש"ס 31d. ירושלמי שם 31e. חזו"א שביעית סימן י' ס"ק ו' 31f. חזו"א שם 32. ד"ה "מן השבת הארץ וכו'"

even if one is not שומר the produce afterwards but are left ownerless their consumption remains forbidden.[27] Concerning produce which do not result from נעבד but have a regular שמירה (the public are prevented from access to them) then their consumption is also forbidden, but only while משומר and not after they have been left ownerless.[28]

Bais Hillel however argue, saying that being נעבד is not a form of משומר and therefore the consumption of נעבד produce is permitted.[29]

Consequently, Bais Shammai forbid the eating of נעבד on account of it being משומר. Bais Hillel permit the eating of נעבד since it is not משומר.[33] This is how the dispute between them is brought in the Mishnayos.[34]

(27) Apparently understanding that on account of being נעבד, a better crop is produced, therefore the effect of נעבד always remains with the crop, unlike the case of משומר where one merely prevented the public from free access to the produce, thus not having an effect on the produce itself.

(28) As far as the actual din of consuming משומר produce is concerned, the Rash[32a] is one of the Rishonim in agreement with Rashi that it can become permitted. See footnote (29).

(29) The Rash has appeared to explain that the dispute between Bais Shammai and Bais Hillel is if נעבד is considered a form of משומר. One will however notice that the Rash,[32b] when discussing the previous drosha "ואת ענבי נזירך לא תבצור" (see above) says clearly that the dispute of Bais Shammai and Bais Hillel in this drosha of והיתה שבת הארץ is in fact whether or not the *consumption* of משומר produce is forbidden, and that the text here should read that it is Bais Hillel who forbid the consumption, so that the drosha of ואת ענבי נזירך לא תבצור will conclude like Bais Hillel. Drosha A forbidding picking משומר even with a deviation (שמורין אסורין בכל ענין), drosha B forbidding picking מופקר only in one way, in the usual manner (ודריש לא תבצור על ענין אחד) This clearly seems to reveal that the Rash understands that consumption of משומר produce is forbidden apparently contradicting what has been said? The Rash in fact retracted from this opinion that consumption of משומר produce is forbidden, on account of the two questions on this view (see above) which he brings.[32c] Therefore when later discussing the drosha of והיתה שבת הארץ and in the Mishnayos,[32d] his view is that consumption of משומר produce is permitted.[32e]

32a. שביעית פ״ח מ״ו 32b. ת״כ ד״ה "ואת ענבי נזירך לא תבצור" ור״ה "אלא על מופקרין" 32c. שם 32d. שביעית פ״ח מ״ו 32e. עיין משנת יוסף ח״ג עמוד קמ״ח 33. שביעית פ״ו מ״א ראב״ד והגר״א על ת״כ 34. שביעית פ״ד מ״ב

Those who learn that נעבד produce is forbidden to be eaten is not a contradiction to Bais Hillel since they pasken like Rabbi Yehudah who says[35] that the text of the Mishnayos reads the other way around, Bais Hillel saying that the produce is forbidden to be eaten.[36]

Theרב עובדיה מברטנורה

The Bartenura in his commentary on a Mishna[37] says that it is forbidden to eat produce which grows by way of having worked the land during Shmittoh. The Bartenura himself, however, does not consider this the primary explanation of the Mishna.

35. שביעית שם 36. עיין בקב ונקי פ״ח הערה כ״ז 37. שביעית פ״ו מ״א

HALOCHOS

OF

SHMITTOH

The pasokim in this section are according to
Hagaon Ha'adir Harav Moishe Sternbuch
references are made to his sefer
שמיטה כהלכתה

CHAPTER ONE

WORK AROUND THE HOUSE AND IN THE GARDEN

1. Which kind of work is forbidden for me to do in my garden and when exactly does this prohibition begin?

Answer: [1] It is forbidden to plough, prune, sow, fertilize or to do any other kinds of agricultural work in your garden,[1] (or in any other area of land in Eretz Yisroel such as a communal park[2]) therefore you must be careful to complete all such work before Rosh Hashona of the Shmittoh year. However with regard to planting fruit bearing trees this is forbidden even before Rosh Hashona—from the 17th of Av (some stop from the 15th of Av).[2] Non-fruit bearing trees can be planted until Rosh Hashona (some refrain from planting these 14 days before Rosh Hashona[3]). You may not graft or layer 44 days[4] before Rosh Hashona if it is done in a way that the fruit it bears will have a din of Orlah.[5] With regard to sowing, some permit it up until Rosh Hashona while others prohibit it from three days before Rosh Hashona.[6]

2. May I sow or plant seeds and flowers in my flowerpots?

Answer: [3] It is forbidden to sow or do any agricultural work[7] in a flowerpot which has a perforation in the bottom or side of it if it is

---

(1) See "Understanding Shmittoh", "Shmittoh in General" Chapter Three no. 3
(2) ibid Chapter Four footnote (4).
(3) (not like חזו״א ibid "Shmittoh in Depth" Chapter Four end of no. 5)
(4) according to the Rambam.[2a]
(5) ibid
(6) ibid
(7) Concerning the exception see question no. 5

placed on the soil or is suspended above the soil outside.[8] Even if the flowerpot has no perforation in the bottom or side of it (so that what grows in it will not draw its nourishment from the ground) it is nevertheless forbidden to sow in it if it is positioned outside on the soil.[9] (Even if the flowerpot is not directly standing on the soil but is suspended by some means above the soil it is forbidden to sow in it.)

Regarding flowerpots which are kept indoors, if one is living in a house or a ground floor apartment where any part of the floor has been left earthen then one may not sow or do any other agricultural work[10] in a perforated flowerpot which is standing or suspended above the earthen part of the floor. However some permi. it if it is a non-perforated flowerpot (except if it is being used for growing a tree in it[11]). Where the perforation in a flowerpot is merely serving as a release for an overload of water in the pot and the hole is so small that a כזית would not be able to slip through it then it has the din of a non-perforated flowerpot.[12] However it is preferable not to sow or plant seeds or flowers even in such a flowerpot.[4] If a perforated flowerpot is standing on the tiled ground floor of a house or ground floor apartment which is directly over the ground then it is permitted to sow in it[5] (and thus do any agricultural work to what is already growing in it). Some however are stringent even in this case because it can draw its sustenance from the grooves between each tile (something which does not apply to an apartment which is

---

(8) See "Understanding Shmittoh", "Shmittoh in Depth" Chapter Three no. 3 and 4.
(9) ibid
(10) Concerning the exception see question no. 5
(11) See "Understanding Shmittoh" "Shmittoh in Depth" Chapter Three no. 4
(12) ibid

---

4. ״אבל ראוי להחמיר שלא לזרוע כלל בשנה השביעית גם בעציץ שאינו נקוב אפילו בבית״ 5. עיין
ביאור ד׳ וכן שמעתי מפי המחבר שליט״א

not directly over the ground[6(13)]).

3. May I sow or plant seeds and flowers in my roof garden?

Answer:[7] A roof garden has exactly the same din as the ground outside,[(14)] in which case any sowing or planting is forbidden during the Shmittoh year.

4. May I plant a miniature tree in a non-perforated pot inside my apartment?

Answer:[8] Concerning trees, then even a non-perforated pot if made of a permeable material such as earthenware has a din of a perforated pot.[(15)] Some authorities are of this view even where the pot is made of wood.[(16)] (See answer to question 2)

5. I have flowerpots with flowers and trees and vegetables which were already sown in them before the Shmittoh year, how am I to care for them during the Shmittoh year?

Answer: Concerning these flowerpots, whether they are perforated or even non-perforated, if they are standing over soil, whether outside or inside, one may only care for them as one does with plants growing outside (see questions 9-19 for details). If they are positioned over a tiled floor inside where the floor is not directly

---

(13) Some [6a] also say that in the case where the tiling is actually attached to the earth beneath it then it is possible that sowing in earth which is on top of this tiling (עציץ נקוב) is considered as actually sowing in the earth under the tiles and would therefore be forbidden. However this would not apply to tiled floors in any apartment not on the ground since the very tiling is completely separated from any earthen ground which might be below it.

(14) See "Understanding Shmittoh" ibid no. 3

(15) ibid no. 4

(16) ibid

8. כן שמעתי מפי המחבר שליט"א 6a. עיין כרם ציון הלכות פסוקות פ"ב הערה ב' 7. פ"א הל' ג' 6. פ"א הל' ד'

attached to the soil,[16a] then one may even sow in them[9a] and all the more so care for them by means of the usual agricultural work. *However*[9] one must be careful in the way he moves around the pots; one may not bring plants growing in a perforated pot (and a tree even in a non-perforated pot made of a permeable material like earthenware or wood) from inside his covered floor apartment to an area outside where there is earth, *even if* one does not place it down but merely holds it in mid-air, because the roots of the plant can draw their nourishment through such a pot from the earth below.[17] Even if the tree, or any other plant, is in a non-perforated pot which is made out of a non-permeable material such as metal, if the branches or leaves are leaning out of the pot and are in line with the earth below then they will draw sustenance from the earth.[18] Therefore one must be careful when moving such a plant onto the balcony, that nothing from the plant hangs over the side opposite an area of earth below.

6. I live in a building which has a communal garden. Some of my neighbours are not very particular about the halochos of Shmittoh, how am I to deal with this situation?

Answer:[10] According to many poskim a person has a mitzvoh dorysa[19] to let *his* land rest,[20] and therefore can be considered as transgressing this mitzvoh even if he himself does not actually do the

---

(16a) See footnote (13).
(17) This is considered a Toldah of זורע (sowing)
(18) See "Understanding Shmittoh" ibid no. 4
(19) ibid Chapter One no. 5
(20) During Shmittoh ones *fruit* and other *produce* is ownerless, but the *land* remains owned.

9a. עיין כרם ציון שם 9. פ"א הל' ד' 10. פ"א הל' ו'

melocha to his land but somebody else does it. Therefore it is necessary for him to make it known to these neighbours that he in no way agrees with them transgressing the halochos of Shmittoh. After such a declaration, even if they do not listen to him, he is not bound to give up his rights to his portion in the garden. However, in order to release himself from all doubts in such a situation, he should declare in front of three people[21] that he makes his rights in the garden ownerless.

7. Does it make any difference if we hire an Arab to do the work in the garden?

Answer: [11] Some of the Rishonim[12] and Achronim[13] are of the opinion that if a non-Jew does work on the land of a Jew during the Shmittoh year then the Jew is transgressing, however they are of the view that if the non-Jew is paid in a way that it is not recognizable that his payment is for work done during the Shmittoh year e.g. he is given a lump sum before Shmittoh for several years work, then it is permissible. One must ask a Sha'alas Chochom.

8. I own an apartment which I have rented out to someone who I have now discovered does not adhere properly to the halochos of Shmittoh and is sowing in the garden, how am I to deal with this situation?

(21) Two act as witnesses, and the third being someone who is able to take possession if he so wishes. This is miderabbonon. Midorysa no one need witness his declaration.

11. עיין בביאור שם 12. תוס׳ רי״ד עבודה זרה טו: אבן עזרא ריש פרשת בהר. 13. מהרש״ל בבא מציעא צ. מבי״ט חלק ב׳ סימן ד׳, מהרי״ט חלק ב׳ סימן נ״ב

Answer: [14] If one has leased the apartment to him for a number of years, including Shmittoh, or he has leased it to him in a way that he cannot evict him, then one must warn him not to do melocha in the garden and by this one has fulfilled his duty, even if the tenant is not prepared to listen.[22] In the case where one is able to evict him, then it is considered as though one is actually leasing it to him during Shmittoh, which is forbidden. However if by the eviction it will cause a large loss of money, or it is not clear that the tenant is doing melocha in the garden, then one must ask a Sha'alas Chochom.

9. May I water fruit trees in the garden?[23]

Answer: [15] If one's intention in the watering is to hasten growth, or to cause the fruits on a tree to become juicier then this is forbidden.[24] If ones intention in the watering is on account of a worry that the fruit tree itself will dry out, then it is permissible but only as much as is necessary.[24a] If there is a worry that *most* of the fruits on a tree will be lost then watering for this need is permissible. If one has no less than ten trees within an area of a *Bais Se'oh* [25] then in the above mentioned cases one may water the earth in the whole

---

(22) Being that the owner is receiving rental money which includes the rent of the garden, he will not want to use the device of withdrawing his ownership.

(23) These are growing in the garden only because they had been sown previously in the sixth year.

(24) Watering plants is a Toldah of זורע (sowing). See "Understanding Shmittoh" "Shmittoh in Depth" "Chart of Agricultural Melochos", "Toldos of זורע" "o". This is therefore forbidden if it is for אבוריי אילנא improving the tree, ibid "Shmittoh in General" Chapter Three no. 8

(24a) Saving a tree from dying אוקמי אילנא is permitted, ibid.

(25) An area of 50 cubits by 50 cubits, one cubit is equivalent to either 48cm (לפי הגרא"ח נאה) or 57.6cm (לפי חזו"א).

area, but if there are less than ten trees then one may only water the actual trees or dig grooves going from one tree to another along which the water may run.

10. What about watering vegetables or flowers? [26]

Answer: [16] Vegetables or flowers which had already been sown and begun growing during the sixth year [27] are treated during the Shmittoh year as just mentioned in question no. 9 i.e. it is forbidden to water them with the intention of hastening their growth or to improve their taste. If the crop is going to die, watering is permitted, but only as necessary.

11. May I water the grass?

Answer: [17] One may not water the grass in the garden every week or two as is usual during the other years. When the grass is losing its shine or there are signs of it drying out, then watering is permitted, but only as much as is necessary. The urgency of the watering is dependant on how hot the climate is and the type of soil involved.

12. May I prune a fruit tree or trim a hedge?

Answer: [18] It is forbidden to prune a tree in a way that it will stimulate the growth or improve the tree. Pruning a vine is

(26) See footnote.(23)
(27) They have no issur S'fichim (see "Understanding Shmittoh" Chapter Six) and therefore may be picked during Shmittoh and used and eaten with *Kedushas Shviyis.*

16. פ״א הל׳ ח׳ 17. פ״א הל׳ ט׳ 18. פ״א הל׳ י׳ וי״א

forbidden even if there is a serious concern that the tree will die without it.[28] However if this is the situation with any other type of tree it is permitted.

Since trimming hedges is normally done for aesthetic reasons and not to stimulate growth it is permitted during Shmittoh. Since some poskim only permit slight trimming to be done in a fashion where it is clear that there is no intention of helping the hedge itself, therefore one should change the way he usually cuts it (e.g. a straight cut at a higher point as opposed to the usual diagonal cut, or visa-versa) and also use a different instrument than usual.

13. May I cut wood from a tree to use for the s'chach of my Succoh?

Answer: [19] This is permissible,[29] *however* some poskim require that the wood must be cut in a way where it is clear that his intention is not to prune it *even if he is cutting from a non fruit bearing tree.* [20] It must be cut in such a way where it is clear that the tree does not benefit.

If municipal gardeners are seen to be cutting trees before chag HaSuccos with the intention of pruning them, you must be careful not to ask them to cut some s'chach on your behalf, because besides causing him to transgress one can also himself be considered as transgressing.[21]

---

(28) Pruning vines is a melocha midorysa "וכרמך לא תזמור" therefore does not have the Rabbinical leniancy of אוקמי אילנא. See "Understanding Shmittoh" "Shmittoh in General" Chapter Three no. 8.

(29) ibid no. 6

19. פ״א הל׳ י׳ .20 אילן סרק 21. שיש שליח לדבר עבירה בשוגג עיין בביאור שם.

14. May I mow the lawn?

Answer: [22] As long as it is only being done for beauty and it is not at the beginning of its growth[(30)] it is permissible. If possible one should deviate from the way he normally cuts it.

15. May I weed the garden?

Answer: [23] No, any melocha like this which improves the ground[(31)] is forbidden. Any melocha which prepares the ground for sowing is also forbidden; this even includes clearing away fallen leaves unless it is done in the manner described in question 16.

16. What about clearing away rubbish scattered around the garden?

Answer: [24] If one clears this away with a broom or with a similar cleaning utensil, so that it is clear that the intention is only for cleanliness and not for the purpose of making it suitable for sowing, then it is permissible.

---

(30) During which time it is usually cut in order to foster its growth (see באור).
(31) See "Understanding Shmittoh" "Shmittoh in Depth" "Chart of Agricultural Melochos" footnote.(6)

22. פ״א הל׳ י״א 23. פ״א הל׳ י״ב 24. שם

17. What about fertilizer?

Answer: [25] One may only put down fertilizer to prevent a tree from dying.[(32)] Even in this case one must only use nitrogenous fertilizer and a limited amount of it. In the case where there is a serious worry that a whole crop of produce will die then the custom is to allow fertilization. However, it is forbidden to bring out the fertilizer from its place of storage to the field at the time of year when fertilizer is usually laid down. One must only do so after this period and also place it in one heap in the field.

18. I want to put up my Succoh in the garden, may I dig holes in the ground in order to rest the poles in them?

Answer: [26] Any digging not done in order to sow, is permissible.

19. May I spray plants with insect repellent?

Answer: [27] Only in a case where there is a definite prospect of trees dying[(33)] or (if not the tree) the majority of its fruits dying from

(32) See footnote (24a).
(33) Footnote ibid.

25. פ״א הל׳ י״ג 26. פ״א הל׳ י״ד 27. פ״א   הל׳ ט״ו

harmful insects may one spray according to the need. One must consult an expert as to whether there is such a need. It is preferable to do all spraying through a non-Jew if he is available. A better alternative to protect the fruits from harmful insects during Shmittoh is to wrap them up.[28]

20. If an area of land needs to be cleared of stones in order to build on it how is one to go about this?

Answer:[29] The builders must first bring the cement and other building requirements and place them next to the site before such clearing is done. This provides evidence that the clearing is not being done to prepare the ground for sowing.

CHAPTER TWO

THE BUYING OF PRODUCTS

Every produce, apart from tree fruit, which grows in the domain of a Jew during the Shmittoh year is permanently forbidden to be eaten.[1](1) One may not even feed them to animals.[2] Some authorities are of the opinion that tree fruits which have not been left for the free use of the public or have had forbidden work done to them are forbidden to be eaten.(2) Therefore during the Shmittoh year fruits and vegetables, etc. must only be bought from shops which have a reliable hechsher. Usually the various Botei Dinim publish pamphlets listing the shops with these hechsheirim. All canned foods and bottled drinks etc. which contain fruits or vegetables must only be bought if they are stamped with a reliable hechsher stating that they are free of any problems of Shmittoh.

There are, however, various problematic situations which one can find themselves in during Shmittoh:

1. If I am in a situation where it is impossible for me to obtain fruits or vegetables with a hechsher what am I to do?

Answer:[3] (a) Concerning tree fruit, if they are the sort which at the time you want to obtain them they have *Kedushas Shviyis*(3) (the various Botei Dinim publicize the dates) then there is a problem that they may have been picked from the field of a Jew who does not

---

(1) For reasons and details see "Understanding Shmittoh" Chapter Six.

(2) ibid Chapter Seven.

(3) Since their חנטה was during the Shmittoh year, see ibid Chapter Five.

1. פ״ב הל׳ ט״ז 2. פ״ב הל׳ ז׳ 3. פ״ב הלכות א־ו

observe Shmittoh. In such a case the fruit may be נעבד(4) or משומר
and some authorities are of the view that such fruit is forbidden to
be eaten.(5) Other authorities are of the opinion that they are not
forbidden to be eaten.(6) Therefore in cases of great urgency, or for
sick and weak people and infants who require fruit for health
reasons, one may rely on the lenient view, *but such fruit may only be
bought in the way explained below in (b).* Healthy people should be
stringent and not buy such fruit.

(b) One is forbidden to do business with fruits having *Kedushas
Shviyis*, or to give an *Am Ha'oretz* money in exchange for them (see
ahead Chapter Five) therefore *when one is in the situation where they
must rely on the lenient view discussed above in (a)* they must
purchase the fruit in the following manner:4

Together with the fruit, one must buy from the seller some other
product which has no *Kedushas Shviyis* and say to him that you wish
him to give you the fruit free of charge but you will pay him more for
the other product and thereby cover the cost of the fruit as well.
However if the other product is so small in value that paying such a
large sum of money for it appears too much like evasion then one
should be stringent that it is business and avoid it, unless there is no
other device and it is an emergency situation.5 *Warning:* This may
only be done in cases of emergency as mentioned above in (a).

(c) Concerning vegetables, then only when it is certain that they
were grown in the domain of an Arab may one buy and eat them.
See below in question no. 2 for details:

(4) ibid Chapter Seven.
(5) This is the custom of those living in Yerushalayim.
(6) This is the custom of those living in Bnei Brak.

2. If an Arab comes to the door selling fruits and vegetables may I purchase them from him?

Answer:[6] An Arab *cannot* be trusted when he says that his merchandise grew in his field or the field of other Arabs, it being a common occurence that Arabs buy produce from Jews and then go and sell them to other Jews.[7]

Therefore one may not buy from Arabs unless it can be proven that the produce was grown in Arab owned fields, e.g. one goes to the Arab market where it is known that most of what they are selling was grown from their own fields a minority being from Jewish owned fields. If an Arab there tells you that what you are buying was grown in one of their own fields, then he may in such a case be believed providing the product that you are buying is a kind which is in the majority of what is being sold there.[7][8]

If one is buying vegetables at the very field of an Arab then it is customary to check that it is his own and not leased out to him by a Jew.

3. Is there any problem in buying material and clothing made with cotton?

Answer:[8] Providing cotton is not in its raw form but has been completely changed then there is no problem. Raw medicinal cotton

(7) During the   Shmittoh year תש״מ it was revealed that Arabs selling bananas (which are considered a fruit and not a vegetable see פ״ב הל׳ ו׳) in the streets of Yerushalayim had purchased them from the Tenuvah Company.

(8) Even though a minority of it might be produce from a Jew nevertheless the rule is that what comes away is considered as having come from the majority.

6 פ״ב הלכות א׳, ט׳, י״ד, ט״ו 7. כיון שבלי דבריו מין הדין כל דפריש מרובא פריש 8. פ״ב הל׳ י׳ ובביאור

(cotton wool) from Shmittoh must not be bought from one who does not observe the halochos of Shmittoh unless one buys it from him using the method described in question 1b. Wood has no *Kedushas Shviyis*[9]and can be purchased as normal.

4. I know that many pills contain starches made from flour or potato , must I buy pills only with a hechsher stating there is none of these ingredients?

Answer:[10] This is a question of debate amongst the Poskim, some are stringent, others are lenient being that the starches only hold the pill together, are unedible even for a dog, and are not eaten in the usual manner. Also they are only swallowed on account of needing a remedy. The custom is to be lenient since their taste is bitter and one has no benefit from the actual eating of them.

5. I am generally meticulous about separating Terumos and Ma'aseros from whatever I buy, even from a store with a hechsher for Terumos and Ma'aseros. Do I need to continue this during Shmittoh?

Answer:[11] If one buys fruits and vegetables[9] during Shmittoh at a time when they have *Kedushas Shviyis* (the various Botei Dinim publicize the dates) then one is not required to separate Terumos and Ma'aseros from them.[10] *However* in the case where one buys

---

(9) Which were sown and began growing during the sixth year.
(10) See "Understanding Shmittoh" "Shmittoh in Depth" Chapter Five no.1.

fruit from an Arab (see question 2 for details), then although produce grown in Eretz Yisroel in the domain of a non-Jew according to some opinions has *Kedushas Shviyis*, and would therefore not need to be tithed like all Shmittoh crops,[11] nevertheless we are stringent and say that there is a requirement for the separation of Terumos and Ma'aseros[12] from such produce. This requirement to separate Terumos and Ma'aseros is only when a Jew does an action to the fruit which completes the way it is going to be finally used.[13] Therefore in the case where one purchases grapes from an Arab, and goes and makes wine or grape juice from them, then one is duty bound to separate Terumos and Ma'aseros from the wine or grape juice. There is a dispute among the Poskim whether one separates Ma'aser Sheni[12] or Ma'aser Ani[12] during Shmittoh, therefore one should say the text of the separation in a way which includes both of these Ma'aseros.

If one buys vegetables at the field of an Arab, he should be careful not to pick it himself because then he will be considered as having done an action which completes the vegetable for use and is duty bound to separate Terumos and Ma'aseros from them.

6. I am in a situation where I find that food prepared for me was cooked in pots which had previously been used for cooking forbidden vegetables. What am I to do?

Answer:[14] One must not eat any food cooked in such a pot if the forbidden vegetables were cooked in it within the last 24 hours. If there are any doubts involved one must ask a Sha'alas Chochom. The pots themselves must be purged before further use.[15]

(11) ibid.
(12) ibid.

12. עיין בביאור שם 13. היינו "גמר מלאכה" ועי' רמב"ם הל' תרומות פ"א ל' י"א לטעם. 14. פ"ב הל' ט' 15. פ"ד הל' י"ב

7. May I buy flowers during Shmittoh?

Answer: [16] Non-fragrant flowers and plants which are used merely for beauty have no *Kedushas Shviyis*, therefore there should be no problem with buying them. However some authorities take the view that even though such flowers have no *Kedushas Shviyis* nevertheless if they were *sown* during the Shmittoh year then it is forbidden to have benefit from them.[(13)] However the main problem in buying them is that it is forbidden to encourage people, who transgress the halochos of Shmittoh, to sow during the Shmittoh year in order to sell the grown products.

Concerning fragrant flowers and plants such as roses and carnations etc. they have *Kedushas Shviyis* and are forbidden to be purchased since it is forbidden to have benefit from such flowers, even to smell them with intention. [17]

8. What about tobacco in cigarettes?

Answer: [18] There is a difference of opinion whether or not tobacco has *Kedushas Shviyis* or is even forbidden to have benefit from. Usually tobacco grown during Shmittoh only enters the market long after the Shmittoh year has ended, and one needs to clarify when this happens. At this time some are careful to only buy cigarettes which do not contain tobacco from Eretz Yisroel.

---

(13) This is because there may apply to them issur S'fichim (ibid Chapter Six). In addition, even those who permit משומר or נעבד are stringent with regard to non-essential items such as flowers.

16. פ״ב הל׳ י״ב 17. כן שמעתי מפי המחבר 18. פ״ב הל׳ י״ב

9. How long after Shmittoh must I continue to be careful about what to buy?

Answer: [19] Vegetables which have been sown during Shmittoh year are permanently forbidden. [14] Grains and legumes which reached a third of their growth during Shmittoh are permanently forbidden. [15] Vegetables which are picked *after* (not during) Shmittoh become permitted from Chanukah and onwards, [16] or when the new crop has come out, even before Chanukah. [17] Consequently, one must always be careful when buying canned products to determine that there is no problem of issur shviyis.

(14) See "Understanding Shmittoh" "Shmittoh in Depth" Chapter Six no. 9.
(15) ibid.
(16) ibid.
(17) ibid.

19. פ״ב הל׳ ט״ז

CHAPTER THREE

HOW TO TREAT FRUITS AND VEGETABLES WHICH HAVE KEDUSHAS SHVIYIS

The custom in Yerushalayim is to consider produce in Eretz Yisroel, which grows in the domain of a gentile, as having *no Kedushas Shviyis*.[1] The custom in Bnei Brak is to consider such produce as having *Kedushas Shviyis*. However, being that there is no *issur S'fichim* regarding tree fruit even if they have grown on Jewish owned land[(1)] and therefore have *Kedushas Shviyis*, we find that whatever custom one has, he is faced with having to be well versed in the halochos of how to treat Shmittoh produce which has *Kedushas Shviyis*. Even though stores with a Shmittoh hechsher usually only supply non-Jewish produce and products from abroad, so that those keeping the custom of Yerushalayim need not treat tree fruit from such stores with *Kedushas Shviyis*, nevertheless one could find themselves in situations where such a store is not available and will have to buy tree fruit which has *Kedushas Shviyis*.

In the following questions and answers "Shmittoh produce" refers to any produce which has to be treated as having Kedushas Shviyis.

1. How am I to treat leftovers of Shmittoh produce on my plate?

Answer:[2] As long as it is still suitable for human or animal consumption then it is forbidden to directly waste or destroy it.[(2)] Therefore one may not throw it away in the garbage can, because by this it becomes foul and thus one has destroyed what was edible.

---

(1) See "Understanding Shmittoh" Chapter Six.
(2) The Torah says that Shmittoh produce is "לאכלה", a drosha is made—to be eaten, but not be wasted.

1. פ״ג הל׳ א׳ 2. פ״ג הל׳ ג׳

One must rather wrap these leftovers in paper, or put them into a nylon bag, after which they may be thrown away in the garbage. This is because one will not be directly causing the destruction of the produce since it will not become fouled by the garbage, rather it will just eventually begin to rot by itself in the wrapping. One should however, try to avoid having to do this by serving an amount of food which will be completely consumed and there will be no need to throw away Shmittoh produce. (See question 3) *However,* if the garbage can is used specifically for putrid wasteage, then it is considered an act of contempt to throw Shmittoh produce into such a place even if it is wrapped up. Therefore, it is the custom in every household to have a garbage can specifically for the disposal of Shmittoh produce; it is referred to as the "Pach Shviyis" (פח שביעית). However, one is still required to first wrap the Shmittoh produce in paper or put it into a nylon bag before throwing it into this Pach Shviyis, since by adding it directly to already spoiling food you are causing its deterioration, which is forbidden as explained before.

One must not empty out this Pach Shviyis into the public garbage can until the Shmittoh produce in the wrappings has rotted. Those who are scrupulous have the custom to set aside two of these Pachei Shviyis, so that by the time the second Pach is full the Shmittoh produce in the first Pach can be assumed to have already become rotten and therefore may be emptied out into the public garbage.[3]

2. May I wash off plates and clean out pots which have scrapings of Shmittoh produce sticking to them?

Answer:[4] One may wash off these tiny scraps *providing* that it is not of a substantial amount where one would normally store it away for

3. עי' בביאור שם 4. פ"ג הל' ד'

further human or animal consumption. In such a case one would have to wrap it up and dispose of it as explained in question 1.

If there are remnants of wilted leaves from Shmittoh produce, and they can with difficulty still be consumed by a person or an animal, then they must first be wrapped up and then thrown in the Pach Shviyis.

3. Is it preferable to cook and serve an amount of Shmittoh produce that I think will not be leftover?

Answer:[5] One should be careful about this.[3] However if one has Shmittoh produce which is not fresh, or is repugnant, or one is already satiated from it, then one is not duty bound to force himself to consume it, and it may be wrapped up and put in the Pach Shviyis.

4. What course of action must be taken when giving young infants Shmittoh produce, such as bananas, which they usually make a mess of?

Answer:[6] If you normally peel for the child a whole banana and he will only eat it like this, then you may continue to do this during Shmittoh. Even if you know that he will leave over some of the banana, or it will become fouled, it is still permitted. What is left of the banana and is not too foul for human consumption must be wrapped up and put in the Pach Shviyis.

---

(3) This is because many Poskim are of the view that one must not even indirectly waste Shmittoh produce.

5. פ״ג הל׳ ה׳   6. שם

If one feels that it is possible to give the child just the amount of banana he requires, then one should do this, and then eat the rest of the banana himself or give it to one of the other members of the household.

5. I have used Shmittoh produce merely as flavouring for soup, meat, or fish. How am I to treat this food?

Answer:[7] Even the taste of Shmittoh produce has all the dinim of *Kedushas Shviyis*. Therefore one must treat the leftovers of this food in the manner prescribed above. (This even applies to water which Shmittoh produce were cooked in)[8] The leftover soup can be left out for one or two days and then be thrown away as usual since by this time it will already have become spoiled.

6. When peeling Shmittoh apples and the like, do I have to be careful to minimize the thickness of the peel?

Answer:[9] One need not be so meticulous and can peel them in the normal manner. However before throwing these peels away they should be wrapped up after which they may even be thrown into the usual garbage can. Orange peels, which today are used for normal consumption (marmalade), should also be regarded as having *Kedushas Shviyis*.

7. What does one do with the pips from Shmittoh produce?

Answer:[9] Some authorities are of the opinion that the pips have *Kedushas Shviyis* like the fruit itself.[4] Therefore, one should wrap them up and throw them in the Pach Shviyis, or one may burn them, providing one benefits from the fire (since large stone pips do not really become rotten, then this is obviously the best procedure)

8. May I puree or extract the juice from Shmittoh produce?

Answer:[10] If it is usual to make puree from the particular species then one may do so as normal.[5] One may squeeze lemons since this is the way lemons are used. However it is a dispute amongst the Poskim if one may squeeze and make juice from oranges and grapefruits. The Chazon Ish is lenient, those who are stringent תבוא עליו ברכה, but in the case of sick and weak people or infants who need such juice one should not be stringent. If this juice has already been made, a healthy person may drink it without worry.

9. Wine and grape juice evaporate when boiled. Is it forbidden to use wine or grape juice, which have Kedushas Shviyis,, in cooking?

Answer:[11] Some say that on account of evaporation it is forbidden.[6] Others say that since cooking improves the wine, it is permitted. Grape juice, which cooking does not improve (because of the preservatives in it) cannot be cooked.

---

(4) They are considered טפל, or minor, to the fruit and take on whatever dinim the fruit itself may have.

(5) The puree is still considered as the fruit itself. Something which is not normally pureed, when it is pureed it is no longer considered as being the fruit thus it has no *Kedushas Shviyis* and therefore one has reduced the size of Shmittoh produce which is considered wasting Shmittoh produce (see ביאור שם).

(6) On account of wasting Shmittoh produce.

9. פ״ג הל׳ ז׳ 10. פ״ג הל׳ ח׳ 11. פ״ג הל׳ י״א

10. May wine which has Kedushas Shviyis be poured into the havdolah cup as usual, so that it spills out, and may one extinguish the havdolah candle in it?

Answer:[12] One must be careful not to let too much wine spill over, and certainly one must *not* extinguish the havdolah candle with it. If one fills up the cup in a way that only an insignificant amount spills out as is usually the case, then if one is anyway not too particular about it, this is possibly permissible.[13]

11. I am scrupulous to use olive-oil for our Shabbos licht. May I use olive oil which has Kedushas Shviyis?

Answer:[14] Since one receives benefit from its light, it is permissible.[(7)]

12. Can I use olive oil which has Kedushas Shviyis for Chanukah licht?

Answer:[15] No, Shviyis olive oil must be utilized, and it is forbidden to benefit from the Chanukah licht.

13. May I apply olive oil which has Kedushas Shviyis to burns?

Answer:[15] No, because olive oil is primarily consumed with food.[(8)]

(7) This is derived from a drosha.[14a]
(8) This is also a drosha.[15a]

12. פ"ג שם 13. עי' בביאור 14. פ"ג הל' י"ב 14a. שביעית פ"ח מ"ב 15. פ"ג הל' י"ב 15a. שביעית שם מ"א

14. I have an apple tree in my garden, the apples on it have Kedushas Shviyis,(9) **what must I be careful about?**

Answer:16 It is forbidden to pick them before they have fully ripened.(10) One may only pick an amount which the head of the family would usually bring home for his household use. One must deviate from the usual manner in which he cuts them off the tree.(11) e.g. Using a knife and not a scissors, or better still to pick them by hand.

The public must have access to the tree. If one is living in an area where persons (or animals)17 are apt to enter and do damage, then it is permitted to lock the access to the tree, *providing* that a sign is put up declaring that the fruit is ownerless and that the key is obtainable. Or the fruit can be given to the "Otzer Bais Din"(12) (אוצר בית דין). Details of how to go about doing this are usually published by the various Botei Dinim in the town.

15. This week I have Arab workers who are repairing my apartment. If they should ask me for some fruit may I give them Shmittoh produce?

Answer:18 Since they are being hired by you for a period of time, then you may give them Shmittoh produce.(13) Had this not been the case then it would be forbidden.(14) If one has an agreement to

---

(9) Because they had their חנטה during Shmittoh, see "Understanding Shmittoh Chapter Five.

(10) This prevents them from becoming fully edible fruits therefore considered causing a loss of Shmittoh produce.

(11) See "Understanding Shmittoh" Chapter Seven.

(12) The produce is put under the jurisdiction of Bais Din.

(13) The Torah 18a says that Shmittoh produce shall be for us to eat and for one who is hired by us.

(14) It is considered wasting Shmittoh produce.

16. פ"ג הלכות י"ג-ט"ו 17. עי' פ"ג הל' י' 18. פ"ג הל' י"ז 18a. ויקרא כה:ו

provide food for a non-Jew then one may give him Shmittoh produce.

16. I have a brother living abroad who has requested that I send him an esrog, may I send him an esrog which has Kedushas Shviyis?

Answer:[19] Normally it is forbidden to send any Shmittoh produce outside of Eretz Yisroel.[15] However if your brother is accustomed to obtaining an esrog every year from a particular orchard in Eretz Yisroel because he is scrupulous about its kashrus, then in this case, where a mitzvoh is involved, it is pemissible.

When travelling abroad, one may take Shmittoh produce as food for the journey.[20]

17. May I use soap or paint which contains Shmittoh produce?

Answer:[21] There is a fear that cotton oil having *Kedushas Shviyis* is mixed into soap Some are therefore stringent to stock up with soap before soap with such a חשש comes on the market.[16] However many are lenient that there is no fear today of soap having *Kedushas Shviyis*. It is customary to use house paint even if it is likely to contain safflower[17] from Shmittoh[18] since the safflower, normally a food, is no longer edible, and therefore loses its *Kedushas Shviyis*. Some doubt this leniency since it appears that nowadays the main purpose of safflower is to be used for paint, and therefore retains its *Kedushas Shviyis*. There is also a problem of נעבד.

(15) One must divest himself of Shmittoh produce at the time of biyur. The Torah[19a] tells us that this can only be done in Eretz Yisroel. Therefore the Rabbonon decreed that Shmittoh produce may not be taken out of Eretz Yisroel.[19b]

(16) When mixed in soap it has not completely lost its form, therefore there is a problem in buying it from one who does not observe the halochos of Shmittoh.[21a] Also it forbidden to have benefit from S'fichim. See "Understanding Shmittoh" "Shmittoh in   General"Chapter Six no. 3

(17) A thistle-like plant yielding a red dye.

(18) It is prohibited to have benefit from S'fichim, see "Understanding Shmittoh" ibid.

19. שם 19a. ויקרא כה:ז 19b. שביעית פ"ו מ"ה 20. עיין ביאור שם 21. פ"ג הל' יח 21a. עיין
פ"ב הל' י'

CHAPTER FOUR

REMOVAL OF SHMITTOH PRODUCE—BIYUR

Tree fruits which have *Kedushas Shviyis* and are permitted for consumption,[1] and vegetables which were sown in the sixth year and were picked during Shmittoh (therefore having *Kedushas Shviyis*)[2] may only be eaten providing the same species is still to be found in the field. After it no longer exists in the field then the Torah[1] commands us to divest ourselves of such crops which are in our possession. A list of dates are published by the various Botei Dinim informing us when the time comes for each kind to be removed.

1. How is biyur done?

Answer:[2] There is no obligation to remove it unless you have more than the amount needed for three meals for yourself, and your family. Whatever is in excess of this must be taken outside and declared ownerless in front of three people (together). They can be your friends who will not take advantage and take possession of it. After this you may immediately regain possession and bring it back into the house. Another method of removal is to take it to an ownerless place and leave it there for a short while even if nobody is around, after this you may take it back home. After re-possessing the produce it still has *Kedushas Shviyis* and must be treated accordingly.

---

(1) See "Understanding Shmittoh" ibid Chapter Six no. 2.
(2) ibid Chapter Five.

1. ויקרא כה:ז 2. פ״ג הל׳ כ׳

2. I was not aware that the date for biyur had come and passed. What am I to do with the produce?

Answer:[3] This produce is permanently forbidden, and it must be burned or buried. One must therefore be careful, when purchasing produce of a species whose date of biyur has passed, that the food is covered by a hechsher.

3. I have food in my possession which has Kedushas Shviyis, however I bought it in the manner described in Chapter Two 1b. Need I worry about biyur?

Answer:[4] Biyur applies as usual.

4. May I make biyur before I am obligated?

Answer:[5] Biyur may only be done on the actual date. These dates are difficult to fix and there are many crops about which we are in doubt as to their actual biyur date. In such cases the Chazon Ish is of the view that one must go through the procedure of biyur daily during the entire period when the doubt exists. Other poskim say that it is only necessary to do biyur during these days on the day that one wishes to actually eat of the produce. They are of the view that if it was not removed on the right date because one had a doubt about this date and wants to eventually remove it then it does not become forbidden to be eaten, since the *main* obligation of removal is only on the final day when there is no longer any doubt that it requires removal and the biyur will again be done on that date also.

3. שם 4. שם 5. פ״ג הל׳ כ״א

5. I have bottles of wine and olive oil which have Kedushas Shviyis. Being that they are no longer in their original form, as fresh grapes or olives, do they have a different time for biyur?

Answer:[6] Their time for biyur is the same as for grapes or olives.

6. I have paints and dyes in my possession. Is there any obligation of biyur?

Answer:[7] If they are the type containing ingredients which require biyur,[3] then they must be removed on the biyur date of the plant they are derived from.

7. I have pickled (or cooked) various Shmittoh produce together so that they all have the taste of each other in them. When the time for biyur arrives for one of them, do I have to remove all of them, since the taste of it is in them?

Answer:[8] You do not have to remove the other produce, *however* if the taste is also in products which have no *Kedushas Shviyis* then since these products will have no time for biyur then they must be removed on the date of biyur of the product which has its taste in them.

(3) Dyes derived from plants whose roots eventually disintegrate require biyur, those whose roots remain do not require biyur (see שביעית פ״ז מ״ב).

6. פ״ג הל׳ כ״ב 7. שם 8. שם

8. I sold a friend of mine a couple of apples[4] which have Kedushas Shviyis. The coins given to me have the Kedushas Shviyis of the apples in them.[5] When the date of biyur for apples comes, is it necessary for me to do biyur on these coins?

Answer:[9] Yes.

9. I keep the custom to consider Shmittoh produce grown in a non-Jewish domain in Eretz Yisroel as having Kedushas Shviyis. Do I have to remove them just like produce grown in a Jewish domain?

Answer:[10] This is a dispute amongst the Poskim. The Chazon Ish is of the opinion that if removal is not done the product becomes forbidden to be eaten. However, this is only if it was in the possession of a Jew.

---

(4) On such a small scale, this is permissible, this not being considered doing business.
(5) See "Understanding Shmittoh" "Shmittoh in Depth" Chapter Five no. 1

9. שם 10. פ״ג הל׳ כ״ד

CHAPTER FIVE

COMMERCIAL DEALINGS

It is forbidden to do business with Shmittoh produce[1] (any produce which has *Kedushas Shviyis*). As mentioned at the beginning of Chapter Three whatever custom one has concerning *Kedushas Shviyis* of vegetables grown in the domain of a non-Jew, one might well buy tree fruit grown in Jewish fields (which are permitted for consumption) which therefore have *Kedushas Shviyis* if they blossomed during Shmittoh. It is forbidden to buy a large amount of Shmittoh produce with the intention of selling them a little at a time to many buyers in order to make a profit, and by each sale he transgresses the prohibition of doing business with Shmittoh produce. It is forbidden for one to buy Shmittoh produce from such a seller since by this one leads him into the transgression.[1(2)]

If, however one sells a small amount of Shmittoh produce in order to use the money to buy food, then some permit this since this is not considered doing business with the produce.

If one did not cut or reap produce but found a quantity of it or was given a quantity as a gift, since he didn't harvest them it is not considered as doing business with them if he sells them. This is providing that one does not sell them in a market or store, since this appears like doing business with them.[2]

If one picks a permissible amount of Shmittoh tree fruit from a garden i.e. enough for a provision for a few days, then he is not permitted to sell them, but another person even a close relative who

---

(1) The Torah[1a] says that Shmittoh produce must be ״לאכלה״ "to eat it". This excludes סחורה, business.

(2) לפני עור.

1a. ויקרא כה:ו 1. פ״ד הל׳ ב׳ וע״י בביאור 2. שם

did not pick them is allowed to sell them. Others say that even the person who picked them and his intention of picking them was on condition to sell them he is allowed to sell them since they were not *purchased* by him but only *picked.* However even in this case they may not be sold in a fruit store but only from a house or courtyard or side street,[3] not the actual market place.

Thus one may purchase Shmittoh fruit from a seller who obtained the fruit in the aforementioned manner.

Another problem,[4] however, is that if the seller is an *Am Ha'oretz* (3) then the Rabbonon decreed that one is forbidden to pay him money the value of more than three daily meals for the fruit. This is because money given in exchange for Shmittoh proudce receives kedusha(4) (the original produce also keep their kedusha) and may only be spent on food and drink(5) (this must also be treated with *Kedushas Shviyis*). An *Am Ha'oretz* might not adhere to this.[5]

1. My only opportunity at the moment is to buy my fruit from a store where they do not observe hilchos Shmittoh. Is there anyway I can deal with this situation? (6)

Answer: [6] It is permitted to give someone Shmittoh produce as a present since this is not considered business.[7] Therefore if you are buying other produce which has no *Kedushas Shviyis*, you can come to an understanding with the merchant that he should give you the Shmittoh produce as a present and you will pay more for the other produce to make up the price. By this method one also avoids the problem of giving money to an *Am Ha'oretz* in exchange for Shmittoh produce, because the money handed over is not being given in exchange for the Shmittoh produce, therefore it does not

(3) A person ignorant of the Shmittoh laws.
(4) See "Understanding Shmittoh" "Shmittoh in Depth" Chapter Five.
(5) ibid Chapter Seven no. 1.
(6) Refer to Chapter Two question 1a, where the problem of משומר or נעבד is discussed. Here only the problem of business with Shmittoh produce is discussed.

receive kedusha.[8] Although the Chazon Ish in such a case forbids this since he views this as also doing business, nevertheless the poskim of Yerushalayim amongst others say that this is not considered business and is permitted. *However*, if the other product is so small in value that paying such a large sum of money for it appears too much like evasion then one should be stringent and consider this as a form of business and avoid it, unless there is no other device and it is an emergency situation.

Another method of avoiding giving an *Am Ha'oretz* money which receives kedusha is to buy the Shmittoh produce on credit.[9][7] *However* some Poskim are of the opinion that even in this case of credit the money payed afterwards, receives *Kedushas Shviyis*, and is only permitted if the debt is paid after the fruit which were purchased have been consumed.

2. Is it permitted to sell Shmittoh produce by weight (so much for a kilogram), volume, or number (so many for the shekel)? Would such a procedure turn it into a business transaction?

Answer: [10] There is indeed such a prohibition and one must only sell Shmittoh produce by *estimating* the weight or volume or number. One may not even use a stone weight which is not precise. However if you stipulate with the storekeeper that he give you the produce as a gift (see question 1) then it is permissible for him to weigh it out. Even produce which has been imported from abroad (and therefore has no *Kedushas Shviyis*) may not be weighed, this is a Rabbinical

---

(7) This is because the money is not being given directly in exchange for Shmittoh produce, but when it is given it is merely to remove a debt.

8. פ״ד הל׳ ו׳ .9 שם .10 פ״ד הל׳ ה׳

decree in order to avoid one coming to mistakenly weigh Shmittoh produce. However in Yerushalayim the custom is to be lenient in shops which adhere to the halochos of Shmittoh since they only sell non-Jewish produce or produce from abroad. When buying from a non-Jew himself who is selling his own produce (see Chapter Two, question 2) there is no prohibition of weighing it, even if one is of the view that they have *Kedushas Shviyis*. Some require that the non-Jew do the weighing.

3. If I am selling Shmittoh produce in the permitted manner, the money I receive has Kedushas Shviyis.(7a) When I buy food with it, may I buy it from an Am Ha'oretz?

Answer: 11 When money having *Kedushas Shviyis* is exchanged for food and drink(8) the money automatically loses its kedusha and what is bought with it receives the kedusha (and must be treated with *Kedushas Shviyis*) therefore there is no problem. This also means that in accepting change from a store-keeper who has coins with kedusha the coins lose their kedusha and you may spend it in the normal way. However there are the few who are careful not to accept change given for a note of money but only for coins, since they are concerned for the view that such notes today are considered שטרות (documents) which cannot make transferences of kedusha. Accordingly the money received for them retains its kedusha. In practice one need not be concerned about this.

(7a) See "Understanding Shmittoh""Shmittoh in Depth" Chapter Five no. 1.
(8) If exchanged for other items (or when given to tzedoka) it does not lose its kedusha.11a

11. פ״ד הל׳ ז׳ 11a. פ״ד הל׳ ח׳

4. If money only loses Kedushas Shviyis if exchanged for food and drink then it means that those who do not adhere to this halocha, and use the money for other purposes, cause markets and banks etc. to be flooded with money having Kedushas Shviyis. Does this mean that when I take out money from the bank or receive change from commodity shops I can only spend it on food and drink?

Answer:[12] The custom is not to be concerned about this. However, some of those who wish to observe Shmittoh in the most perfect manner set aside some food worth a p'ruta and say "any money or items having *Kedushas Shviyis* which is in my possession should be transferred onto this food". This food is then treated as *Kedushas Shviyis*, and the money and items can be used as normal.

5. If I am eating in a restaurant which adheres to the halochos of Shmittoh but I treat non-Jewish produce as having Kedushas Shviyis and also do not do business with it, is there anything I must be careful about?

Answer:[13] There are no problems as far as payment is concerned if you pay the bill *after* you have eaten the meal (see end of answer to question 1). In order to avoid the problem of business you should stipulate that you will only pay cost price for the produce which you eat without giving him any profit[9] adding instead to the money paid for the non-Shmittoh items. However in the case where you do

---

(9) Since no profit is accruing it is not considered business.

not eat the food before payment e.g. you order food for a Bar Mitzvah or wedding etc then you must stipulate that the produce received is a gift and the payment for the non-Shmittoh items can be at a higher price to compensate for it.

Payment for work done with Shmittoh produce also is considered as doing business with Shmittoh produce. Therefore the cook can only be compensated for the time he could have spent doing something else, but not for the actual cooking (שכר בטלה).

6. If I am buying Shmittoh produce from a non-Jew do I have to be careful when giving him money in exchange just like I do when giving it to a Jewish Am Ha'oretz?

Answer: [14] The Chazon Ish is of the opinion that the money in this case does not receive kedusha. Some Poskim like the Shl'oh, however, have a custom to be stringent and view the money as receiving kedusha, and when buying Shmittoh produce from a non-Jew one must first make a קנין הגבהה (lift them at least one to three טפחים in the air with the intention of acquiring them), stipulating that he will then pay money in order to remove the debt incurred by this acquisition. Payment can then follow immediately. Others have a custom to give him the money while whispering to themselves that the money is a present.

7. I have a hardware store. I suspect that some of the customers do not adhere to the halochos of Shmittoh. Are there any garden tools etc. which I must not sell to them?

Answer: [15] Tools which are difficult to determine whether they are to be used for permitted melocha or not are forbidden to be sold to

14. פ״ד הל׳ י״א 15. פ״ד הל׳ י״ב

such people. Some say that there is no fear of this causing ill feelings since one is not bound to sell his wares, others disagree.

8. What about lending them household utensils such as a sieve and a grinder?

Answer: [16] Since refusal might lead to ill feeling therefore the Rabbonon allowed one to lend them such things if it is possible to assume that they are to be used for permitted melocha even though it might be a farfetched assumption e.g. a sieve could be used for counting money therefore we attribute this as his intention for borrowing it. One should not lend them things such as pots and pans or cutlery which are used with heat. If one has lent them these utensils then before using them again one must purge them.

9. Is there anything I need to be careful about when hiring labourers to do permitted work with Shmittoh produce?

Answer: [17] It is permitted for labourers to do permitted work with Shmittoh produce e.g. to reap a permitted amount of fruit, and the salary one gives them for this work receives no *Kedushas Shviyis*.

However if they decide to cut more than the permitted amount and in their transportation of it they do not work by the hour[18] but they charge for a job[19] (which is much more expensive) then the Rabbonon decreed as a fine that the salary they receive for this has *Kedushas Shviyis* thus limiting them to spend it only on food and drink.[19] One should therefore in paying them stipulate with them that it is for non-Shmittoh work, the Shmittoh work being free, and thus the money given to them has no *Kedushas Shviyis*.[20] This fine was also given to those who do jobs of painting using emulsifying paint containing oil with *Kedushas Shviyis*.

16. שם 17. פ״ג הל׳ י״ג 18. שכיר יום 19. קבלנות 20. עי׳ בביאור

GLOSSARY

Achronim: Later authorities (from fourteenth century onward)

Amora: scholar of the Talmudic period

Amoroim: scholars of the Talmudic period (Third through fifth century C.E.)

Am Ha'oretz: a person ignorant of Shmittoh laws

Am Yisroel: the Jewish nation

Asmachta: a verse which the sages of the Talmud use to base their prohibition on but not that the verse itself is revealing this prohibition

Av Melocha: father—primary melocha

Bais HaMikdosh: Temple in Jerusalem

Bais Din: Jewish Court of law

Bavli: Talmud compiled in Babylon

Beraisa: Tannaic statement which was not included in the compilation of the Mishnayos by Rabbeinu Hakodosh

Biyur: Removal of Shmittoh produce

Bnei haYeshiva: disciples of the Amoroim

*Botei Dinim:*plural of Bais Din

Botzer: picking grapes

Bovel: Babylon

Chachomim: sages

Chazal: sages (of the Mishnaic or Talmudic period) of blessed memory

Chazoka: acquisition gained by virtue of use or habitation

Chidush: an innovative understanding of a Torah subject

Choresh: ploughing

Derabbonon: Rabbinical law

Din: law

Dorysa: Torah law

Drosha: method of deriving laws from Torah verses

Eretz Yisroel: the land of Israel

Gemora: Talmud

Gezera Shova: derivation based on comparing two Torah verses containing the same word

Halocha: accepted law

Halochos: accepted laws

HaMelech: the king

Har Sinai: Mount Sinai

Hechsher: Rabbinical certification of kashrus

Hechsheirim: plural of Hechsher

Hekdesh: Temple property

Hekesh: derivation based on comparing two parts of a Torah verse or two adjacent verses or topics

Issur: prohibition

Kabbola: tradition

Kedusha: sanctity

Kedusha Rishona: first sanctity

Kedusha Shniya: second sanctity

Kedushas Ha'oretz: the sanctity of the land

Kedushas Yerushalayim VehaBayis: the sanctity of Jerusalem and the Temple

Kivush: conquest

Kodesh: holy

Kohen: descendent of Aharon, who Hashem charged with the responsibility of carrying out the service in the Temple

Kotzer: reaping of grain or legumes

Levi: person from the tribe of Levi

Malkus: fourty-nine lashes dealt out by Jewish court

Meleches Machsheves: work done with purpose

Melocha: form of work, either primary (Av) or derivative (Toldah)

Melochos: plural of melocha

Miderabbonon: from Rabbinical law

Midorysa: from Torah law

Mikdosh: Temple in Jerusalem

Mishkon: Tabernacle which housed the Schechina during the Wilderness period

Mishna: tannaic statements included in Rabbeinu Hakodosh's compilation

Mishnayos: plural of Mishna

Mitzvoh: Biblical or Rabbinical injunction

Mitzvos: plural of mitzvoh

Mizbei'ach: altar

Moshe Rabbeinu: Moses our teacher

Motzoai Shmittoh: the year following Shmittoh

Parsha: a section of the Written Law

Pasken: make a halochic decision

Perek: chapter

Poskim: those who give halochic decisions

Posuk: verse

P'sak: accepted law

P'sukim: verses

Rabbonon: Rabbinical authorities

Rishonim: early authorities (eleventh to fourteenth centuries C.E.)

Sefer: sacred book

Sha'alas Chochom: question to a Rabbinic authority

Shechina: Divine Presence

Shofar: ram's horn that is blown on Rosh Hashona

Talmidim: pupils

Tanna: a scholar of the Mishnaic period (First and Second century C.E.)

Tannoim: scholars of the Mishnaic period (First and Second century C.E.)

Toldah: offspring—derivative of principle melocha

Tosefes Shviyis: period of prohibition of melocha preceding and in *addition* to the Shmittoh year

Yerushalmi: Talmud compiled in Jerusalem

Yom Din: day of judgement
Yom Tov: Jewish holiday
Zomer: pruning
Zore'a: sowing seeds